Memory Crafting
Beyond the Scrapbook

Judi Kauffman

krause
publications

700 East State St., Iola, WI 54990-0001
Telephone (715) 445-2214
www.krause.com

Please call or write for our free catalog of publications. Our toll-free number to place an order or obtain a free catalog is 800-258-0929 or please use our regular business telephone 715-445-2214 for editorial comment and further information.

Library of Congress Catalog Number: 99-61441

ISBN: 0-87341-795-X

Printed in the United States of America

Photography by Rick McCleary
Photo styling by Orange Potter, Esq.
Author photo by Debra Donovan

Dedication & Acknowledgments

I believe in the inherent creativity of all people. I received the gift of this belief from my parents, Joseph and Sara Gichner, and my grandparents, Rose and Sam Fisher and Samuel and Tina Gichner.

This book would not have been possible without Tanya, who pushes and challenges me, and Jo, who calms me. Nor without my second mother Sonya Gichner, my friends Kathy, Anita, Marie, and Suzanne, who always listen.

The talented Orange Potter provided props, assisted with styling, and let me use his fabulous costumed photographs featured in Chapter 10. Rick McCleary, my photographer and long-time friend, made an overwhelming task into a happy adventure.

I am forever grateful to Jacqueline and Andrew Kreinik and Ruth Schmuff, who launched me.

The support I have received from friends within the craft and needlework industry has been fantastic. Each time I needed tools, supplies, and moral support they came forward. Thank you Lisa, Kathleen, Diane, Ed, Mary Jo, Paul, Witt, Margaret, Cilene, Karen, Julie, Marie, Nancy, Amy, Solange, Tom, Karen, Diana, Fred, Rhonda. A special thanks to Husqvarna Viking for providing a Viking 1+, the sewing machine of my dreams, and to Xyron for the laminating machine.

Two talented people at Krause Publications, book editor Barbara Case and designer Jonathan Stein, brought the pages to life through their hard work and energy.

If I am beginning to sound like an actress on Oscar night, it's because the list is long and heartfelt.

Most of all, thank you Frank! You believe in my creativity and you give me space in every meaning of that word. You stand beside me with your arms and your heart open. The memories I cherish most are the ones we share.

Introduction

When I turned forty and needed reading glasses, I bought funky blue half-frames with a small row of rhinestones at each side. My friend since third grade, Anita, burst out laughing. I was indignant. After all, we were born on the same day so she'd surely need them soon too. When I asked why she was laughing, she went to her closet and pulled out a tattered photo album with a picture of me taken at age nine wearing - you guessed it - blue glasses with rhinestone corners. Not only did she share the memory in those wonderful recesses of her brain, she had "evidence" to show our husbands and her daughters.

Memories are powerful bonds we build with friends and family and within our own hearts. If you are like me, there is a box in your closet filled to bursting, moved from house to house and state to state, or stashed away in the place your family has called home for generations. Mine contains the newspaper announcements of my engagement and wedding, brittle after thirty years; pictures of me and my friends, smiling teenagers crammed into a beachfront photo booth; letters from students who sent words of praise or support over the years; and a wide variety of memorabilia too precious to toss away. It's a magic box with special powers. Memories spill out every time I peek inside. In those photos I am a young woman eager to start the adventure of marriage. In those letters I find a teacher trying to unlock the creativity of the students who appear in her classes. What a shame we didn't know then what we know now about preserving memories. The acid from the tape I used ate anything it touched and the pressed flowers fell apart.

There is a bigger box in the basement with fabric and lace, buttons and labels. It contains my family history. I've always called them "visual remnants" because each piece recalls a garment made by my mother, grandfather, or by me. It, too, is a magic box with special powers. In those pieces of brocade and wool, I am once again a teenager on the way to the prom, a young woman dressed for a job interview. When I touch the buttons, I am nine years old again, playing with them at my grand-mother's house.

Each of us has treasures saved over the years. They differ from person to person. The fabric scraps that conjure up days spent making special clothing might look like rags to anyone but their owner. The collection of Christmas cards that bring love from around the world make no sense to a minimalist who doesn't want more than one kind of mustard in the refrigerator at any given time.

To those of us who save and savor, these special treasures are valuable and irreplaceable.

I had a wonderful time exploring my memories as I designed the projects for this book. I was transported to my childhood - my grandmother's cinnamon rolls and stew fragrant in the background, the feeling of my grandfather's smooth strong hands as he taught me to sew, the hugs and celebrations as I gained confidence and skill. All came flooding back as I looked through handwritten recipe books and boxes of fabric scraps.

I sorted the neckties my husband Frank, my father, and my cousin Norman gave me when I started working on the chess and checkerboard, remembering occasions when the ties were in style and in favor. I think all three men were happy to see me reduce their hoarded castoffs to small squares of silk. I have saved the most garish for Halloween costumes or joke gifts.

I felt grateful and reverent when friends offered to share their memories by giving me photographs, handkerchiefs, old linens, fabrics, and pieces of lace. My friend Charles shared vintage photos and family stories while we looked through the special treasures that had been stored in the barn in Virginia. I love the notion of rescuing something that was damaged and giving it a new life.

There are so many occasions to celebrate and so many reasons to create something special as part of the fun. We who love to craft, knit, crochet, sew, and stitch, hardly need an excuse to get out our supplies and make something.

Big events like weddings and anniversaries call for special albums, a cover for a video, an elegant picture frame. But little events like the first two-wheel bike ride are worthy of celebration too.

When a baby is born, any self-respecting grandmother is going to make a blanket - whether it be an heirloom christening blanket to be passed from generation to generation, or a humble prequilted fabric "blanky" with a story written between the lines (dragged till it shreds, worn out from being loved).

And what about when a friend or colleague deserves words of praise? An embellished certificate might be just right. And what should I do with that stack of travel brochures and postcards I've collected? And all of those fortune cookie fortunes I just couldn't bear to throw away? And the labels from hundreds of skeins of embroidery floss? Some of those floss labels in the collector's cabinet (Chapter 2) are from projects I stitched with my mother when I was a child. Are you a pack rat too?

I'm hooked. I love creating cherished memories from things I've saved for a long time and letting the new "stuff" I acquire become the focus for more ideas.

It's such a treat to step into my studio and see what happens. With all of the wonderful new products like affordable laminating machines, specialty scissors and paper punches, photo transfer paper, inks that dry in seconds, and more, I don't think I'll ever run out of things to make.

Welcome to my first book. It has been a labor of love and I hope you enjoy it.

Judi Kauffman

Contents

Chapter One
Materials, Tools & Techniques

I hope you will find within these pages lots of projects to make for yourself and for the people you love. Because I've been a teacher for thirty years, I've tried to be very specific about what you need to do to have your project duplicate mine whenever possible. At the same time, you won't have exactly the same stash of old hankies or the same vacation memorabilia, nor will your yard have the same leaves and ferns, so I've given directions for how to customize and change the designs. That way, you can create something to suit your taste, budget, and décor.

I made many of the projects in more than one way to help you think with "fresh eyes" - to look at each project as a starting point. For example, the Trio of Trees in Chapter Six is shown as a 3" square Christmas ornament, as an 8" pocket for a tote bag, and as a large wall hanging. You could also make it as a bed-sized quilt (lots of blocks or a jumbo center medallion), or even smaller to wear as a pin.

If the supplies I've suggested aren't available at your local craft or needlework store, contact the manufacturers listed in the Resource Guide and they'll help you find a source. Or substitute what you have on hand.

My fondest hope is that the "What Else" idea list with each project will lead you in new and different directions and that each suggestion will spark even more ideas. Asking "What Else" starts an internal dialogue full of possibilities

and takes a project beyond your first and most obvious thoughts into fantastic, creative areas you hadn't imagined. I like to ask myself, "What if I only have an hour?" to see if I can make a quick version of a project. Or "What if I want to change the colors?" "What else can I do with those stamps or threads or paper scraps?" and so on.

For example, make a paperweight using ticket stubs from plays or sports events, or use stamps from the cards and letters you receive at holiday time instead of the lace and sequins I chose for my paperweights in Chapter Two. Or make the button jar autograph project featured in Chapter Five into a wall hanging instead of a pillow.

My favorite books are the ones I can return to, each time glad that I brought them home. I hope this one becomes an old friend, visited over and over. Write in the margins, tape things to the pages - use this book like a favorite cookbook that gets sticky and stained where the recipes you like best can be found.

Dip into your attic and closet, open those boxes and savor the feelings that the contents evoke. Mix together some tears and some smiles, a little acid-free glue, some thread, elegant paper, and fabric.

Use this first chapter as a reference for the rest of the book. Pick a project, jump right in, and have a wonderful time!

Tools & Materials

Good quality tools and materials make projects easier. I bought three pairs of my favorite scissors to keep in different work areas, a luxury that has saved me many steps. I own a Xyron machine for laminating and for making stickers, another luxury that I now enjoy on a regular basis. My Fiskars paper crimper makes me smile every time I take it out. Whatever your budget, whether you work on the kitchen table or in a designated studio room, invest in the best tools and supplies you can find and afford, then organize them in a way that works well in your space. They will serve you long and well.

Each project lists the items needed. When I have given a general description like "seed beads" rather than a color number, it is so you can choose beads that go with your fabric or collectibles. The rest of the time I have been very specific, listing brand name and item number. If you aren't able to find an item at your local craft or needlework shop, please substitute what you have on hand or use the Resources at the end of the book listing manufacturers' addresses and phone numbers. They will help you find a store or mail order source. Always follow manufacturer's directions, including all safety precautions.

The Xyron machine is a big investment, often available for use at a store that specializes in scrapbooking, but a tool that might be worth sharing with a friend - you'll use it for making stickers, laminating place mats, mounting photographs, and so much more.

The tools and supplies listed here are my studio basics and the products used throughout this book.

✦ For cutting - Fiskars Razor Edge scissors, paper crimper, paper edgers, and 45mm rotary cutter with decorative, plain, and scoring blades. I use the En Garde shield on my rulers to protect my hands.

✦ Mini-hole punch - McGill 1/16" hole punch.

✦ To remove button shanks - Pliers with spring from JHB International.

✦ Laminating and adhesive application - Xyron 850 and 1250.

✦ Glues, coatings, and finishes - Fabri-Tac, Gem-Tac, Kids Choice (craft glue), and Liquid Laminate from Beacon Chemical Corp.; Therm-O-Web double-faced adhesive sheets; Liquitex matte acrylic medium; Brush Strokes from ADI; EnviroTex Lite pour-on coating from ETI.

✦ Sewing machine - Viking 1+ from Husqvarna Viking.

✦ Sewing and machine embroidery threads, embroidery floss, over-dyed French wool, metallic braids and ribbon, crochet yarns - Anchor, J&P Coats, Coats and Clark, Kreinik Manufacturing Co., Inc., Needle Necessities, DMC.

✦ Ribbon - Artemis Exquisite Embellishments, Bucilla, Sweet Child of Mine.

✦ Pillow inserts - Soft Touch from Fairfield Processing.

✦ Batting and fusibles - Fun-dation, Quilt-Fuse, quilt batting, Crafter's Choice fusible stabilizer, Trans-Web paper-backed fusible webbing from HTC/Handler Textiles.

✦ Milwaukee heat tool #1400

Additional supplies are listed with each project.

Photo courtesy of Fiskars.

Photo courtesy of Xyron.

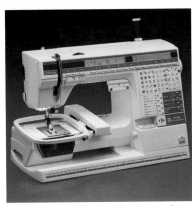

Photo courtesy of Viking Sewing Machines.

Glues & Adhesives

My goal is simple - if I stick it on, I want it to stay on. There are many wonderful glue and adhesive products on the market. Make sure you match the product to the task. Read the label. Wear latex surgical gloves from the pharmacy if your skin is sensitive or if you want to keep your manicure perfect. Otherwise, get messy and keep a nail brush by the sink.

To attach a slick item like a flat-backed metal piece, button, or plastic lizard to paper, wood, or fabric, you need jewelry glue (like Beacon Gem-Tac).

To attach paper to paper, fabric to paper, or paper or fabric to wood, you need double-faced adhesive sheets (like Therm O Web Peel n Stick or Coats Instant Stick & Hold) or craft glue (like Beacon Kids Choice). Or use the adhesive cartridge on the Xyron machine. You can also use an all-purpose fabric glue like Beacon Fabri-Tac.

To attach fabric to fabric or buttons to fabric, use fabric glue like Beacon Fabri-Tac. To fuse fabric to fabric, use a paper-backed iron-on product like Trans-Web from HTC/Handler Textiles.

Pillows, Wall Hangings, Mats & Runners

There are hundreds of ways to finish pillows - ruched sides, knotted cording, box pillows, and more. I have used a basic knife-edge pillow throughout the book, adding ruffles or gathering the corners to get a different look. Explore other books on sewing techniques if you want to finish your pillows in a more elaborate way.

Pillows

1. Cut backing fabric to match size of pillow front.
2. Baste or pin piping or ruffle 1/8" from seam line and machine sew it to pillow front.
3. With right sides together, sew pillow front and back together around all sides, leaving an opening on one side.
4. Gather corners for a soft-cornered pillow (see the Taj Mahal pillow on page 42). For other pillows, clip the corners. Turn right side out.
5. Put pillow insert into cover. Close the opening with small, invisible stitches. Or put a seam or zipper in the back or overlap two hemmed fabric pieces as an envelope and use back access for putting insert in pillow.

Wall Hangings Are Pillows Without Stuffing

1. With right sides together, sew front and back together, leaving an opening on one side.
2. Clip corners, turn right side out, and close the opening.
3. Sew hanging loops in the top seam when attaching front to back. Alternatively, turn back hems at top and bottom to form casings. Hang from dowel or decorative hardware.
4. Add a fusible stabilizer like Crafter's Choice to the back to keep wall hanging smooth or baste quilt batting to wrong side of front piece for a soft quilted project.

Table Mats/Runners Are Wall Hangings Without Hanging Loops or Casings

1. Baste quilt batting to wrong side of front piece for a quilted project.
2. With right sides together, sew front and back together, leaving an opening on one side.
3. Clip corners, turn right side out, and close the opening.

Knife edge pillow - A

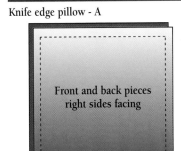

Front and back pieces right sides facing

Leave open

Clip corners

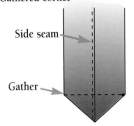

Turn right side out. Insert pillow and stitch opening closed.

Gathered corner

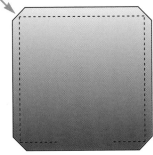

Side seam

Gather

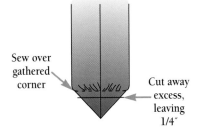

Sew over gathered corner

Cut away excess, leaving 1/4″

Knife edge pillow - B (envelope back)

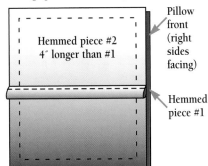

Hemmed piece #2 4″ longer than #1

Pillow front (right sides facing)

Hemmed piece #1

Sew all four sides. Clip corners. Turn right side out.

Ruffled pillow

Right side pillow front

Corner can be rounded or squared

Wall hanging - A

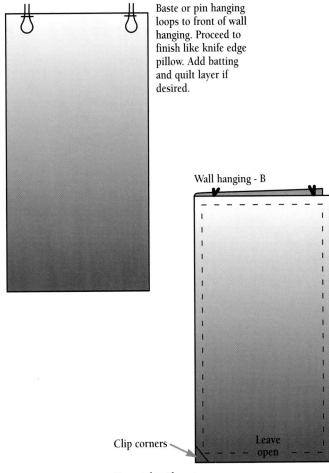

Baste or pin hanging loops to front of wall hanging. Proceed to finish like knife edge pillow. Add batting and quilt layer if desired.

Wall hanging - B

Clip corners

Leave open

Turn right side out
Close opening with small stitches

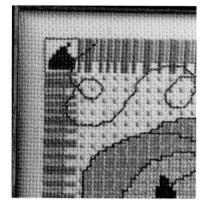

Cross-Stitch Basics

Cross-stitch is worked with a blunt tapestry needle that glides through the holes in the fabric without splitting either the fabric or threads in adjacent stitches. Each pattern specifies what kind of fabric to use based on a thread count which determines how many stitches will fit in a given space. It also specifies what kind of thread to use and how many strands.

Before stitching with more than one strand, separate the strands (they come in 6-strand skeins) and reassemble the bundle before threading the needle so the strands lie side by side and smooth instead of twisted. This is called "stripping," not to be confused with exotic dancers or printers who have entirely different jobs by the same name.

Each stitch is a small X made of two diagonals, crossed over each other in the same direction every time. Cross-stitch patterns often call for straight lines called backstitching to define and accent areas or to create lettering and fine linear details.

Each color has a different symbol on the color key. Each square on the chart equals one stitch, unless otherwise noted. Sometimes there are beads, buttons, bows, or other embellishments added. Each will be indicated on the chart and color key.

To change and customize a cross-stitch project, change both the thread count of the fabric and the number of strands and kind of threads used - the size of the project will enlarge or reduce dramatically, depending on what you decide.

Many people keep fabric taut on an embroidery hoop, frame, or stretcher bars. Others work with fabric soft, rolling it to hold steady. Always bind or zigzag the edges of fabric so they won't unravel or snag threads while you work.

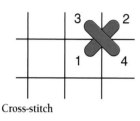

Cross-stitch

Backstitch

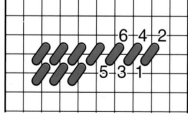

Needlepoint Basics

Needlepoint is worked with a tapestry needle with a blunt point that glides through holes but doesn't split threads. There are no knots on the back of needlepoint. Instead, the thread tail is anchored at the beginning of a new color or length of thread by holding it at the back of the canvas and stitching over it for about an inch to secure it. At the end of a length of thread or when changing colors, slide the needle under four or five stitches on the back of the work, pull the thread through, and cut it close to the exit point.

Work with a piece of thread, yarn, braid, or raffia approximately the length of your forearm (15"-18"). Long pieces fray and tangle.

Tent or Continental Stitch

Each stitch is a short diagonal covering the intersection of two threads. Since the projects in this book are worked on rigid plastic canvas, the "threads" are rows of plastic. Work stitches following the diagram at left.

Overcast

To overcast edges, hold ribbon or thread at an angle to cover plastic. At outer corners, stitch three times in the same hole to make sure plastic doesn't show.

Tent or continental stitch

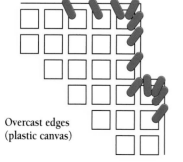

Overcast edges
(plastic canvas)

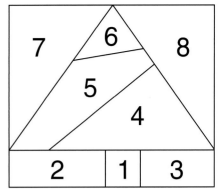

Trace lines and numbers on Fun-dation material.

Foundation Piecing

Foundation piecing is an easy technique that looks like complex patchwork but does not require templates, patterns, or precise sewing. You add fabric scraps one at a time in the order marked on a foundation block traced on translucent material especially made for foundation piecing. It's as easy as one, two, three…

Some people sew onto paper. In fact, you often see the technique called "paper piecing." I find sewing on paper frustrating - paper dulls the sewing machine needle and I can't see what I'm doing, plus you can't leave the paper inside a project to stabilize it. I recommend Fun-dation translucent quilt block piecing material from HTC/Handler textiles.

Remember, since you are building the block from the wrong side of the marked foundation, the finished block will be the **reverse** of what appears on the drawn lines. Give yourself a bit of time to practice and absorb the technique. It is easy to do once you have tried it, but it feels awkward to everyone at first.

Set the sewing machine stitch length to 12 per inch. If the foundation will not be left inside the project as a stabilizer (soft quilts or garments), set the stitch length to 18 per inch so it can be easily torn away. Projects can be pieced by hand if desired.

1. Using ruler and pencil or fine line permanent fabric marker, trace the block (lines and section numbers) on Fun-dation translucent quilt block piecing material.

2. Cut a piece of fabric large enough to cover section #1 of the block, plus enough to extend at least 1/4" on all sides. Pin this fabric **wrong side up** to the back (unmarked side) of the Fun-dation. This is the only piece pinned wrong side up. All remaining pieces are added right side up, right side facing the right side of the previous piece. Note: You will be stitching on the lines on the marked side of the Fun-dation, but the fabrics are added on the unmarked side, underneath.

3. Turn block over. Place fabric for section #2 on top of section #1, **right sides together**, so both edges overlap the printed line between the two sections. Be sure fabric #2 is large enough to cover section #2 plus a generous 1/4" allowance. To check placement before stitching, fold fabric #2 out to its right (finished) side to be sure it covers section 2 and has seam allowances all around.

Hint for Beginners: Think of the fabrics, face to face, as butterfly wings that are closed. After you sew on the guideline, the fabrics will open side by side like butterfly wings.

(continued on next page)

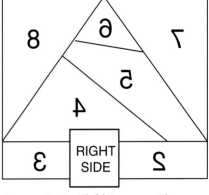

Cover section 1 with fabric, wrong side against back of block.

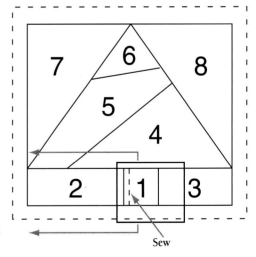

Working from right (front) side of block, add fabric for sections (in numerical order) face up under the previous section. Sew along line and open fabric out to cover numbered area.

Complete foundation piecing instructions are packaged with Fun-dation Translucent Quilt Block material from HTC.

4. Turn the Fun-dation over, returning to the side with numbers and pattern. Place the block under the presser foot of your sewing machine with the Fun-dation side up. Start stitching just before the printed line. Stitch directly along the line and stop one or two stitches beyond the line. For stitches that meet the edge of the block, stitch just past the dotted cutting line.

5. Turn over. Carefully trim seam allowance to scant 1/4". Fold fabric #2 to the right side to cover section #2 on the Fun-dation. Press along seam line.

6. Add fabric #3 to cover section #3, aligning it right sides together with fabric #2. Check its placement to assure full coverage of section #3 and stitch along the line between sections #2 and #3. Trim seam allowance and press.

7. Continue adding fabrics in numerical order until the block is completed. Baste or pin in seam allowance. Cut on dotted line.

8. Finish according to project instructions.

Ribbon Embroidery

Silk ribbon embroidery is dimensional, soft, and lush. Use a chenille needle when stitching with silk. This type of needle has a sharp point to pierce fabric and broad shoulders to open a hole through which the ribbon can slip as you stitch. Cut pieces no longer than 18" unless instructions specify otherwise.

Needle Threading

Ribbon will slip out of the needle with each stitch unless it's locked on each time you add a new piece. Thread the ribbon through the eye of the needle three or four inches. Turn the point of the needle and pierce the ribbon about 1/2" from the end. Turn the needle upright, holding it near the point. With the other hand, pull the ribbon straight down. Lock the little tab (the part that was pierced) down over the eye of the needle. A shortcut to remember - "Thread and pierce, pull and lock."

Ribbon Knotting

Fold the tail of the ribbon toward you about 1/4". Pierce the fold with the point of the needle. Pull it down over the needle. Continue pulling down, forming a large soft knot

Boat Leaf

Thread a sewing needle with thread to match the ribbon. Fold the ribbon in half. Follow the diagram on this page. Use a running stitch to gather the leaf from one end to the other. Adjust the gathers and tie off the thread. Open and flatten the leaf.

Rolled and Gathered Rose

Thread a sewing needle with thread to match the ribbon. Fold one end down and across to form a bud. Gather the bud. Continue to gather and roll the ribbon, securing it at the base after every few inches of gathering. Stitch at an angle to create final petal, gather, and secure the thread. Keep the base flat (see the photos on page 15).

Note: For an extra lush folded edge, use wide ribbon folded in half lengthwise. Stitch through both layers as you work. The rose made of Artemis hand-dyed bias cut silk on page 28 has a folded edge.

Gathered Petal

Thread a sewing needle with thread to match the ribbon. Sew a running stitch like the letter U. Gather and secure the thread. Tuck the raw edge under another flower or embellishment (see diagram on page 15).

Boat Leaf

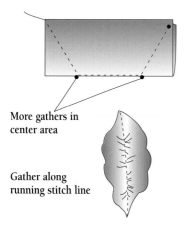

More gathers in center area

Gather along running stitch line

Needle Threading

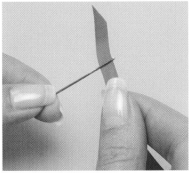

1. Thread ribbon through eye of needle three or four inches.

2. Turn point of needle and pierce ribbon about 1/2″ from end.

3. Turn needle upright, holding it near point. With other hand, pull ribbon straight down.

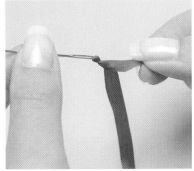

4. Lock little tab by pulling it down over eye of needle.

Gathered Petal

This edge will be top of petal

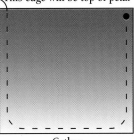
Gather

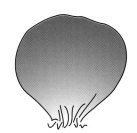

Gather along running stitch line

Step-by-step photos courtesy of Bucilla

Rolled and Gathered Rose

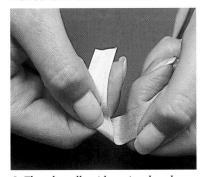

1. Thread needle with sewing thread to match ribbon. Fold one end of ribbon down an angle, leaving tail to use as handle.

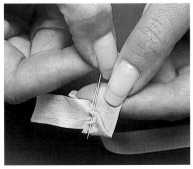

2. Fold ribbon back across itself. Stitch three or four running stitches along bottom edge.

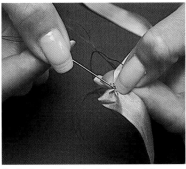

3. Gather to form bud. Secure with one or two stitches at base.

4. Continue to make running stitches, two or three inches at a time, gathering ribbon while twirling it around itself. Secure at base as you go. The longer the ribbon, the fuller the flower. Make last few running stitches cross end of ribbon at an angle to form final petal.

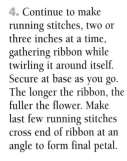

5. Stitch several times so flower won't pull out. Cut off excess ribbon.

Japanese Ribbon Stitch

Bring the ribbon up through the fabric. Smooth it in the direction of the stitch. Turn the needle upright and pierce the ribbon in the middle at the point where the stitch will end. As you pull the ribbon through itself, hold it smooth and let it curl around your finger. Pull the ribbon gently from the back of the fabric until the stitch turns inward and forms a point.

1. Bring ribbon up through fabric and smooth it in direction of stitch.

2. Turn needle upright and pierce ribbon in the middle.

3. As you pull ribbon through itself, hold it smooth and let it curl around your finger.

4. To control point of stitch, turn fabric over to pinch ribbon between thumb and forefinger. Return to surface and watch the end turn inward. Pull gently to control point at end. Stop when it looks right.

5. The completed stitch.

French Knot

Bring the ribbon up through the fabric. Turn the needle parallel to the fabric and wind the ribbon away from you and back toward you one or more times, keeping it tight enough to form a small round shape (but not too tight to pull the needle through). At the same time, turn the needle upright and insert the point back into the fabric very close to where you came up. Hold the ribbon tail while you pull the needle to the back of the fabric. Let go of the ribbon when it begins to disappear. The finished knot is soft and full.

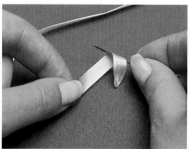

1. Bring ribbon up through fabric. Turn needle parallel to fabric and wind ribbon away from you and back toward you around needle one or more times.

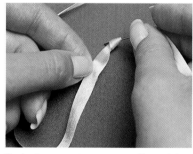

2. At the same time, turn needle upright and insert point back into fabric very close to where you came up.

3. Hold ribbon tail while pulling needle to back of fabric. Let go of ribbon when it begins to disappear.

4. Don't pull too tightly so the needle can slip through.

5. The finished knot is soft and lush.

Violet

Thread a sewing needle with thread to match the ribbon. Make two petal sections, one with three petals and one with two. Sew the two-petal section to the fabric to form the upper portion of the flower. Sew the three-petal section slightly over it to form the lower portion. Sew a French knot or beads at the center.

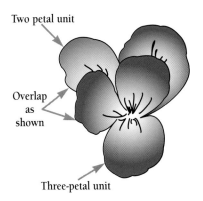

Two petal unit

Overlap as shown

Three-petal unit

Violet

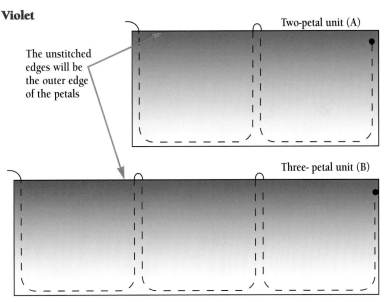

Two-petal unit (A)

The unstitched edges will be the outer edge of the petals

Three- petal unit (B)

Make one two-petal unit (A) and one three-petal unit (B)

Shawl Collar Petals/Leaves

Thread a sewing needle with thread to match the ribbon. Fold the ribbon to mark a center point. Fold the sides over each other at an angle. Gather with a running stitch across the base. Cut off the excess. Tuck the raw edge under another flower or embellishment.

1. For petals and leaves that end in a point, fold a piece of ribbon at an angle like a shawl collar.

2. With matching sewing thread (we show a contrast so you can see), sew a running stitch line across the base.

3. Gather the petal, tie off the thread, and cut off excess ribbon.

4. Sew in place.

5. Hide the raw edge under a button, bead, or flower.

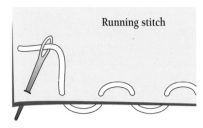
Running stitch

Running Stitch

Begin with a single straight stitch. Continue making straight stitches, keeping the length of each stitch and the distance between them even.

Feather stitch

Feather Stitch

Work toward you. Insert the needle to the right of the starting point. In a scooping motion, bring the point of the needle up through the fabric below the center of the two points, forming an open loop that looks like a V. Make another stitch, this time inserting the needle to the left of the starting point. Repeat, alternating right and left starting points until you have as many stitches as needed. Secure the final loop with a small straight stitch at the point of the V.

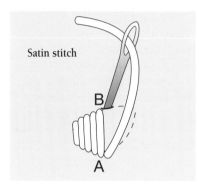
Satin stitch

Satin Stitch

Make straight stitches, side by side, with each one beginning on one side of the shape and ending on the other. Repeat parallel stitches until the shape is filled.

French Knot

The French knot for embroidery is worked the same way as for ribbon embroidery. Follow the instructions on page 16 and substitute floss or wool for ribbon.

Stem Stitch

Draw a guideline if needed and begin with a straight stitch. Start each subsequent stitch at the halfway point of the previous one. If the line changes direction along a curve or circle, change the starting point of each stitch from the inside of the line to the outside of the line.

Floss & Crewel Embroidery

Use embroidery and crewel needles. Work with thread that is no longer than your forearm to keep it from fraying or tangling. If a pattern calls for more than one strand, separate them and put them back together before threading the needle to keep them side by side and smooth.

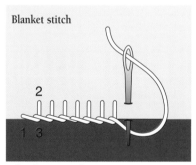
Blanket stitch

Blanket Stitch

Bring thread up through the fabric, hold it to the side, and in a scooping motion, take needle behind the fabric and bring it back up into the loop formed by the thread. Repeat the stitch, keeping the distance and length the same each time. Right handed people work left to right, lefties work the opposite direction. To stitch on a curve, angle the lines as needed.

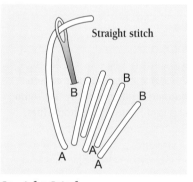
Straight stitch

Straight Stitch

Bring thread up through the fabric. Smooth it with your finger and insert the needle where you want the stitch to end. Straight stitch lines can be long or short.

Etceteras

Tea-Dyed Lace and Fabric

To give a vintage look to fabric or trim, soak them in strong tea for half an hour. Rinse, dry, and iron the fabrics. Raspberry tea will give a soft pinkish tint - soak for an hour. If possible, lay fabrics flat in the tea so the color is absorbed evenly. A glass pie dish is good for small pieces.

Removing Button Shanks

Always protect your eyes with goggles or glasses when removing button shanks and keep children and pets out of the way because small plastic or metal pieces may fly off. Use pliers with a spring to cut the shanks close to the back of the button. File the back of the button to rough it up, remove little stumps of the shank, and to give glue some extra texture to grab.

Photocopies and Photo Transfers

A careful copy center will enforce copyright laws, saying you can't copy from a book. There are three projects for which the author and publisher give you rights to make copies for personal, noncommercial use - the recipe cards, certificates, and message squares. That means you can copy, decorate, and give away as many as you want, but you can't sell them.

Many projects call for iron-on transfers. I photocopy my "art" onto sheets of Photo Effects from Hues, Inc. Any copy center with a color copier can do this. There are also products for creating transfers on a home computer. Copyright laws apply to color transfers. Leaves and other botanicals, lace, collage, photographs that you have taken yourself (not ones in books or magazines), and printed matter designated copyright-free (like the Dover book series) are okay to copy for transfers.

Collage & Composition

When project instructions say "arrange the postcards as shown in the photograph or as desired" or suggest that you "move the elements until you like the arrangement," I'm asking that you create your own composition. The collectibles and mementos you use in your projects will be different from mine, so it's important that you feel confident. Until you glue something in place, it can be moved again and again while you decide what you like. I often leave a project on the table for a day or two before committing myself to the final arrangement. When I look at a design after a break, I often change, add, or remove something.

Composition Options

1. **Arrange things in rows** and see if you like the effect. A grid structure (orienting elements in lines) is a sure-fire way to make things look simple and elegant. The objects don't have to match in size; in fact it's fun to have something much larger or something that's an unusual color, just for contrast. The shell pillow is a good example of a formal grid.

2. **Make a symmetrical composition.** The round lace paperweight is a good example. By having two halves or sides match, the composition is stable.

3. **Work with asymmetrical balance.** Place things on the diagonal like the postcards in the memory tray.

Diagonals give movement to a composition, keeping your eye moving around. Check out the coat rack with two little mittens on one side, balanced by a large mitten on the other; or the foundation pieced heart with a swag of flowers on one side.

The Project Buffet

TREAT THE CHAPTERS FOLLOWING this page as a buffet where you can pick and choose what to sample first.

Just like at a buffet where you get to choose your favorite things, if you have a favorite technique, you can start with the projects that feature it. Sometimes it's fun to taste something new and different at a buffet, so be adventurous and try a craft you've never done before.

Or simply browse through the pages till something tempts you. If you like to eat several desserts at a buffet (as I do), consider your favorite project to be dessert and make a lot of different versions. I could probably make Backyard Botanical greeting cards (Chapter Ten) for years without getting bored - Mother Nature provides the best buffet of all.

Every project is designed to give you lots of options for turning the things you save, collect, and treasure into something unique amd memorable. Whether you create a sewing box for someone just learning to stitch or a T-shirt for a family reunion, a memory tray, keepsake envelope, or quartet of satchets - I hope you find the projects a delicious buffet you return to often.

Chapter Two

Under Glass

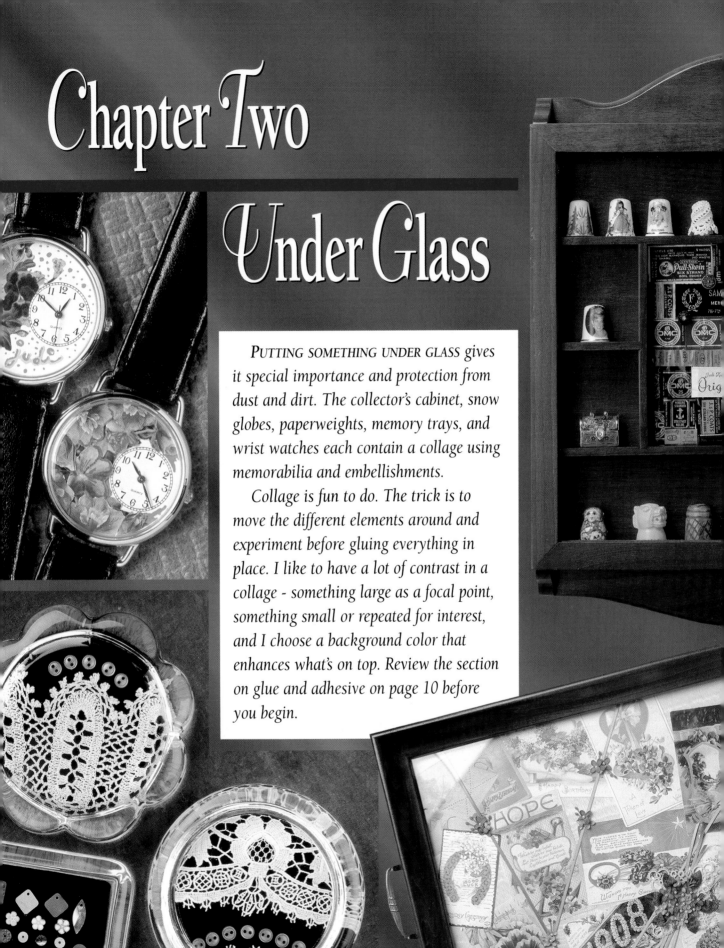

PUTTING SOMETHING UNDER GLASS gives it special importance and protection from dust and dirt. The collector's cabinet, snow globes, paperweights, memory trays, and wrist watches each contain a collage using memorabilia and embellishments.

Collage is fun to do. The trick is to move the different elements around and experiment before gluing everything in place. I like to have a lot of contrast in a collage - something large as a focal point, something small or repeated for interest, and I choose a background color that enhances what's on top. Review the section on glue and adhesive on page 10 before you begin.

My Favorite Things

Create a collage of small-scale memorabilia to display with your collectibles. I chose buttons, labels, and embroidery floss wrappers to create a collage for my thimble collection. Choose things for your collage that match your treasures.

Assemble
✦ Collector's cabinet from Sudberry House
✦ Acid-free glue, gem glue
✦ Double-sided adhesive sheet
✦ Acid-free board
✦ Small-scale memorabilia, both flat and dimensional
✦ Tracing paper (optional)

How To
1. Review information on glues and adhesives (page 10) and removal of button shanks (page 19).
2. Cut board to fit display area of cabinet. Cut double-sided adhesive sheet to cover board.
3. Cut piece of paper the same size. Arrange memorabilia on paper. Trace the design to remember exact placement.
4. Working with the bottom layer first, reassemble the collage on the adhesive-covered board. Use glue to add remaining layers and dimensional elements.
5. Put the collage into the cabinet and display your treasures on the shelves.

What Else
✦ Create a collage for each season. Cut notches in two sides of the collage so it can be easily removed and replaced. Put holiday ornaments, acorns, and other items that go with the collage on the shelves.
✦ Make a photo collage and display mementos on the shelves. If you collect shells, use beach photos and shells in the collage. If you're making a gift, make a collage with photos of the recipient and display miniatures from favorite hobbies and shared events.
✦ Design a mini-collage for the background of each shelf in addition to the center area. Each can be for a different stop on a vacation, family member, or event. Display souvenirs on the shelves.

Shake It Up Baby

I was so excited when I found snow globes that could be customized with a photo, collage, or needlework insert that I bought a dozen of them. They make wonderful, inexpensive instant gifts. Who can resist the pleasure of shaking a globe to watch glittery snow drift down? Keep them on desk or dresser to make you smile.

The liquid and glitter are in front of a small, flat slot where your collage will remain dry and clean.

Assemble
✦ Snow globe from Yarn Tree
✦ Double-sided adhesive sheet
✦ Jewelry glue
✦ Card stock
✦ Photograph
✦ Inside globe - small flat buttons, flowers, or other embellishments
✦ Outside globe - dimensional embelishments

How To
1. Remove base, foam, and manufacturer's insert from globe.
2. Cut card stock piece to fit. Create a small flat collage on double-sided adhesive sheet with photo(s) and embellishments.
3. Insert collage in the slot in the globe. Attach the base.
4. Using jewelry glue suitable for slick surface, attach embellishments to the globe's exterior.

What Else
✦ Make a globe for each family member, display them as a group at a reunion or holiday gathering and let each person take one home.
✦ Instead of using photographs, make a mini-collage with theater tickets, a reduced-size photocopy of a report card, collectibles like buttons or lace, or an award ribbon.

Little Pleasures

A paperweight is both useful and an object of beauty. Like other projects in this chapter, the paperweights are collages made of small-scale objects. Glass and acrylic paperweights are available in many shapes and sizes, ideal for bits and pieces of salvaged or leftover lace, tiny buttons, or sequins.

While the items you choose will dictate the background, remember that black velvet makes an elegant background for anything light and delicate.

Arrange the items in rows, arcs, or angles. Overlap and layer if you prefer.

Assemble

✦ Paperweight designed for needlework or collage insert (glass paperweights from Yarn Tree)
✦ Lace, buttons, sequins, or other small flat memorabilia
✦ Background fabric or paper
✦ Acid-free craft, gem, or fabric glue

How To

1. Remove cardboard insert from paperweight. Cut fabric or decorative paper same shape as insert and glue it to cover insert.
2. Arrange items as desired and glue in position.
3. Reassemble paperweight with cork backing.

What Else

✦ Place beautiful fishing lures on muted green velvet.
✦ Incorporate single earrings or small pieces of broken costume jewelry.
✦ Make a collage of tiny photographs.
✦ Combine pieces of fabric, beads, and trim from special sewing projects like weddings and proms.
✦ Write a message by hand or on the computer, or cut a section of a greeting card and use it as the background for your collage.

Memory Trays

I love bringing tea and cookies to the table on a handsome tray. It transforms a casual visit with friends into a special event. A tray near my sewing table holds small scissors and spools of thread - the handles make it easy to carry things from room to room when I work on projects. You'll think of lots of reasons to make memory trays.

I chose vintage postcards for my trays. If the items are valuable and shouldn't be cut or glued, you may want to use color copies for the collage instead of originals.

Assemble
+ Memory tray from Sudberry House
+ Fabric or paper (to cover cardboard insert that comes with tray)
+ Collectibles up to 1/4" high (narrow ribbon, flowers, buttons with shanks removed)
+ Acid-free glue
+ Tracing paper (optional)

How To
1. Remove cardboard from tray. Cover with fabric or decorative paper.
2. Arrange collage on paper, cut to tray size. Trace the design to remember exact placement.
3. Starting with the bottom layer, glue everything in place on covered board.
4. Assemble the tray, using spacers along edges so glass doesn't squash the dimensional embellishments. If insert is to be permanent, add felt (provided by manufacturer) to back of tray. To change inserts, attach felt with Velcro strips to give access to back of tray.

What Else
+ Create welcome, holiday, or party theme tray inserts. Change them to surprise friends and family.
+ Assemble a farewell or congratulatory tray as a group project. Include photographs, flowers, and good wishes. Have everyone sign the collage in gold pen.
+ Honor a special teacher by surrounding a class photo with messages, autographs, and other memorabilia.

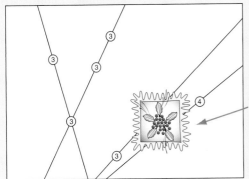

Lace motif with leaves and flowers

Lines = 1/8" ribbon
③ = Three-flower cluster
④ = Four-flower cluster

Timely Treasures

Glance at your wrist and find a photo of loved ones, a collage of beads or stickers, a favorite flower, or a tiny painting. And find out what time it is too! These watches were specially designed for embellishment.

Assemble
✦ Watch with snap-off crystal from National ArtCraft
✦ Tiny photographs, beads, buttons, stickers (as shown or as desired)
✦ Markers
✦ Acrylic paints and fine paint brush
✦ Acid-free glue
✦ Sharp fine-point scissors
✦ Compass
✦ Toothpick or corsage pin
✦ Tweezers (optional)

How To
1. Remove crystal from watch, following manufacturer's directions.
2. On piece of paper, use compass to draw a circle the same size as the watch face with a smaller circle where the hands and numbers are. This area must remain free of dimensional decoration, but can be painted.
3. Cut sections of photographs, flowers from catalogs, or trim stickers and arrange them so they fit. Do not remove backing from stickers until you place them on the watch face. Overlap things as needed.
4. Use toothpick or corsage pin to apply tiny amount of glue to each element as you position the design on the watch face, and to move things into

position. Use tweezers to hold small pieces while you work. Let glue dry.
5. Write or paint words or pictures as shown or as desired.
6. Reassemble the watch.

What Else
✦ Make a "best friends" watch with faces from photos of several people.
✦ Make a "new baby" watch for proud grandmothers.
✦ Use rubber stamps to create a design.
✦ Make a miniature color copy of a child's drawing.

Chapter Three

Weddings, Anniversaries & Special Occasions

THE BIG EVENTS IN OUR LIVES include weddings and anniversaries, milestone birthdays, and other special occasions. The projects in this chapter commemorate and celebrate these happy days, but there's no reason not to make them just for fun.

Love Is The Foundation

The secret to this elegant project is a very simple technique called foundation piecing. No templates, no cutting precise pieces to fit together! You use fabric scraps that are bigger than the section they are going to cover, then trim away the excess.

The technique is described on page 13. Remember, you add pieces of fabric **under** the piece of translucent quilt block piecing material where you have traced lines and numbers.

Beginners should think of the fabric pieces as butterfly wings. When they are closed, they are face to face (right sides together). When they are open, they are side by side and form a symmetrical mirror image. Each piece you add starts out under the one you

previously added, like closed butterfly wings. Follow the numbers and what looks like precise patchwork takes shape.

Trust me. Try it. And if you goof, try again. It is only awkward until you get the hang of it. Make sure you check out the trio of trees on page 74 that uses the same technique.

Assemble
✦ Fun-dation translucent quilt block piecing material from HTC (square piece the size of finished project - as shown, 13" block framed as 12" panel)
✦ Fabric scraps for heart, contrasting fabric scraps for background
✦ Sewing and machine embroidery

thread in colors desired
✦ Two yards 2½"-wide Artemis hand-dyed silk ribbon (choose color to coordinate with fabric pieces for this and organza ribbon)
✦ Two 6" pieces 2½"-wide organza ribbon
✦ Velvet leaves and buds from Ruban et Fleur
✦ Three heart or other charms
✦ Seed beads and metallic thread in colors shown or as desired
✦ Pencil or fine line permanent marker
✦ Ruler
✦ Iron and press cloth
✦ Backing board, batting, frame (optional)

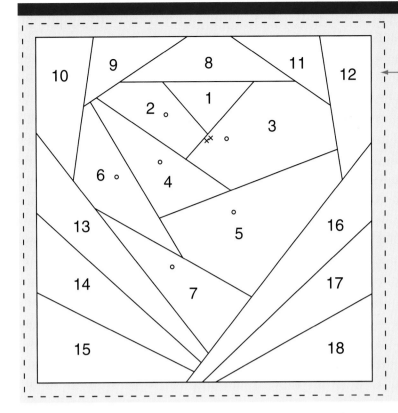

← 1/2" seam allowance

○ Pieces 2 to 7 = Heart
Pieces 1 + 8 to 18 = Background
× = Charms

Cut finished block on dotted line

How To

1. Enlarge and trace pattern, including lines and numbers, on Fun-dation material. Include dotted cutting line for seam allowance and finishing. Note with an * which pieces are background so you remember when to change colors.

2. Following foundation piecing directions on page 13, piece the heart block.

3. Embellish the seam lines within and around the heart with machine embroidery in a contrasting color. I chose a soft gray in keeping with the Victorian look. As shown, stitches are on the A, E, and F cards of the Viking 1+.

4. Refer to ribbon directions on page 14 and make a large rose from silk ribbon and two gathered petals from organza.

5. Wrinkle the velvet leaves along the wire to add dimension. Sew them in place with seed beads along center line and metallic thread, doubled in needle, at sides.

6. Sew silk rose, organza petals, and charms in place.

7. Back with batting and cardboard, then frame.

What Else

✦ Hand embroider crazy quilt stitches along the seam lines within and around the heart.

✦ Embellish with purchased silk flowers instead of making them.

✦ Finish as a pillow.

✦ Make a larger block for a banner, medallion quilt, or wall hanging; a smaller block for the lid of a box, pin cushion, or sachet.

✦ Use country fabrics for a pot holder and matching apron pocket, or make a series of blocks for a lap throw or bed quilt.

✦ Select animal prints or pastels for a baby or child's room.

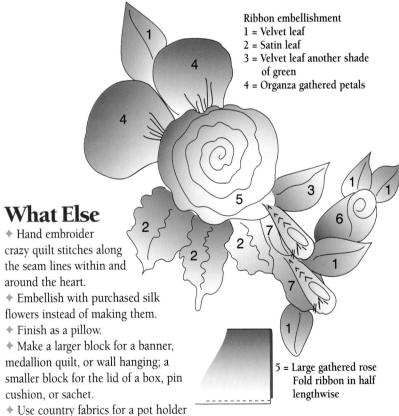

Ribbon embellishment
1 = Velvet leaf
2 = Satin leaf
3 = Velvet leaf another shade of green
4 = Organza gathered petals

5 = Large gathered rose
Fold ribbon in half lengthwise

6 = Shawl collar petal "bud" with raw edge tucked under leaf

7 = Purchased vintage or velvet bud or fruit

Corner Quartet

I found a beautiful handkerchief at an estate sale. It had fine embroidery on each corner but also had small stains and a hole. I decided to rescue it to honor the person whose handwork would otherwise be tossed aside, and the person who once used and cherished it.

I cut the hankie into four pieces to make four sachets. The corners in perfect condition received minimal embellishment - just a few beads. The damaged areas got lots of embellishment to hide the flaws. Because the hankie is sheer and fragile, I backed each section with a piece of fabric. I used contrasting color fabric as backing for two of the sachets to show through the open work and tint the background.

Find a vintage hankie or pretty pieces of fabric or cut sections from old napkins or other embroidered linens to give them a second life.

Assemble

✦ Vintage handkerchief or other embroidered material/linens
✦ Lining and backing fabric (velvet, moiré, cotton)
✦ Sewing thread to match fabric and beads
✦ Bead needle
✦ Mill Hill seed beads, leaves, and flowers as shown or as desired
✦ Vintage or tea-dyed lace and lace flowers
✦ Ruffled organza ribbon
✦ Lavender, dried rosebuds, or other fragrant sachet filling (approx. 2 cups per sachet)

How To

1. Cut hankie or fabric into squares. Baste sheer fabrics to matching or contrasting fabric for stability and to conceal threads used to attach embellishments.
2. Sew beads, lace, flowers, and other dimensional elements in and around embroidered areas or cluster them over stains and holes.
3. Make each square into a little pillow. Fill with lavender, potpourri, or add fragrant oil to fiberfill. Refer to page 10 for directions on making a pillow.
4. Sew ruffle into seam allowance or add trim at edge after sachet is complete.

What Else

✦ Back fabric pieces with fusible batting and fill with sand for a paperweight or pincushion.
✦ Connect squares to make a pillow, lap throw, wall hanging, baby or bed quilt. Sew plain fabric squares between embellished ones or add fabric strips to enlarge them.

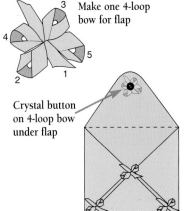

Use halfway point on inner square to determine corner points on outer square

Square 1/2" larger than keepsake

Add 1/2" seam allowance on all four sides

Keepsake and booklet

Make three 2-loop bows

Keep right side of ribbon facing up on all loops and tails

Gather at center with matching thread

Make one 4-loop bow for flap

Crystal button on 4-loop bow under flap

Keepsake Envelope

Many families have one special keepsake, passed from generation to generation. It may be a watch or a Bible or a handkerchief used by each bride. Make this keepsake envelope to hold such a treasure. Record names and dates in a matching fabric-covered book or on a card kept in an acid-free vinyl sleeve and tuck it inside the keepsake envelope. The history accompanying the keepsake is a treasure too.

Keepsakes need not be expensive heirlooms. A lucky penny or souvenir pin can merit a fabric envelope too.

Assemble

✦ Fabric for envelope and lining (see diagram to determine amount)
✦ Matching sewing thread
✦ Ribbons and button for embellishment (as shown or as desired)
✦ Paper, pencil, ruler
✦ Fray checking product

How To

1. Lay object and optional notebook on paper. Draw a square or rectangle around them. Following diagram, extend lines to form envelope flaps. Add 1/4" seam allowance.
2. Cut two pieces of fabric for envelope and lining. Refer to page 10 for directions on making flat mat or wall hanging.
3. Fold bottom and side flaps up and use tiny stitches to sew them together with matching thread.
4. Make three single and two double bows, following diagram. Apply fray checking product to diagonally cut ends. The right (shiny) side of ribbon will show on both loops and tails. Sew three single bows to center and sides, then double bow plus vintage button to lining side of flap, taking care not to stitch through outer layer of envelope fabric. The bow and button inside flap

hold it in place. If you prefer, they can be on outside front of flap.
5. Size of bows will be determined by size of envelope. An envelope 6" when folded (as shown) uses 1/2"-wide ribbon. Use wider or narrower ribbon accordingly.

What Else

✦ Make an envelope for each attendant at a wedding. Include a small gift with a copy of the invitation.
✦ Send fabric envelopes to everyone invited to a celebration and ask them to bring it filled with photographs or other mementos. After the event, make a wall hanging with an envelope sewn to each section.
✦ Change the look from elegant to funky by making envelopes in plaid flannel with a leopard lining or black and white stripes lined in a lime green print.

Happy Couple Needlepoint Cake

A whimsical wedding cake for the bride and groom. This needlepoint project will take less than an evening because many of the stitches cover lots of canvas at a time. It's easy enough for a beginner and the plastic canvas needs no blocking.

Assemble

✦ Embroidery floss, metallic ribbon, and braid listed in color key
✦ Tapestry needle
✦ 14-count plastic canvas
✦ Bride and groom teddy bear buttons from JHB International (with shanks removed) or other embellishment for top of cake
✦ Craft glue
✦ Greeting card, magnet, frame (optional)
✦ Synthetic suede (for backing a magnet)

How To

1. Review basic needlepoint and embroidery instructions on page 12.
2. Stitch needlepoint cake. Embroider icing and decorations.
3. Cut around stitched cake and plate, leaving one row of plastic on all sides and two small unstitched plastic extensions to hold bride and groom buttons steady. Omit extensions if project will be mounted. Enlarge extension as needed for magnets with larger embellishments.
4. Overcast edges with metallic ribbon held at an angle. Stitch three times at outer corners to cover plastic.
5. To finish as magnet, glue synthetic suede and magnet to back of cake. Use small amount of glue so it won't seep through. Glue bride and groom buttons to unworked plastic tabs at top of cake.
6. To frame, glue to decorative paper or board, mat, and place in shadow box.
7. For a greeting card, glue to front of card and mail in padded envelope to protect embellishments.

What Else

✦ Choose different colors, stitch only the bottom layer, and add candle buttons for a birthday cake.
✦ Use a different mesh plastic canvas for a bigger cake. With 1/2" fabric strips stitched on 5-count plastic, miniature stuffed animals can be used for the bride and groom.
✦ Replace bears with small rosebuds, doves, or a wire-edged ribbon bow.

Pattern on page 34

With This Ring

There's something special about a ring box. Maybe it's that old saying about good things coming in small packages. Both of these little boxes are easy to make. One is needlepoint on a square of plastic canvas that needs no blocking. It takes less than an evening to complete. The other is fabric padded with quilt batting. It takes only minutes.

Assemble for Needlepoint Box

✦ White wash ring box from Sudberry House
✦ Kreinik metallic ribbon, braids, silk floss listed in color key
✦ Sweet Child of Mine silk ribbon listed in color key
✦ Tapestry needle
✦ 14-count plastic canvas
✦ Craft glue

How To

1. Refer to general needlepoint instructions on page 12.
2. Complete stitching. Cut out square, leaving one row of plastic on all sides.
3. Overcast edges with metallic ribbon held at an angle. Stitch three times at corners for good coverage.
4. Glue completed square to ring box lid.

What Else

✦ Substitute colors you prefer and change the look of the box. For example, use only white, ivory, gold, and tan for a tone-on-tone effect.
✦ Use embroidery floss instead of silk.

Assemble for Fabric Box

✦ White wash ring box from Sudberry House
✦ Small scale print fabric
✦ Quilt batting scraps
✦ Twisted cord

✦ Silk flowers, velvet or silk leaves
✦ Dove (JHB International #20060) or other romantic button, shank removed
✦ Craft glue
✦ Needle and thread

How To

1. Cut four pieces of quilt batting same size as cardboard insert that comes with ring box. Stack and lightly glue to each other and to cardboard.
2. Cut square of fabric 1/2" larger than cardboard. Using sewing thread doubled in needle, stitch running stitch around fabric and gather it over padded cardboard (like a shower cap).

Tie securely.
3. Glue padded square to box lid.
4. Starting at one corner, glue twisted cord around lid. Glue twisted cord bow over corner where twisted cord joins. Glue on silk flowers, leaves, and dove button. Refer to photo for position.

What Else

✦ Add a charm shaped like a cross and use the box for a rosary.
✦ Choose velvet or satin and make a Victorian ring box.
✦ Replace the twisted cord with lace for a ruffled edge.

Pattern on page 34

Include two unworked canvas tabs
for bears when cutting out canvas

Project instructions on page 32

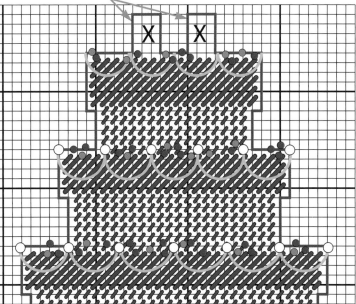

Anchor Floss - 6 strands

- ● #204 Green ⎤ French knots, 6
- ● #51 Pink ⎦ strand floss doubled in needle
- ✎ #1 White
- ✎ Kreinik #16 med braid #001 Silver
- ── Kreinik #16 med braid #001 Silver - overcast edges of plate
- ── Kreinik 1/16" metallic ribbon #032 Pearl - overcast edges of cake

Kreinik #16 med braid #095 Starburst

○ = 3mm pearls, Sulyn Industries, Inc.

X = Bear button or other embellishment

Project instructions on page 33

✎ Kreinik 1/16" ribbon	045 Confetti Gold	
⫽ Kreinik #16 med braid	2829 Seafoam	
⫽⫽ Kreinik Soie d'Alger	3323 Mauve	
✎ Kreinik Soie d'Alger	1324 Red Purple	
✎ Kreinik Soie d'Alger	545 Yellow Orange	
✎ Kreinik Soie d'Alger	244 Yellow Green	
Petals Silk Ribbon	Green Leaves	

Design by Judi Kauffman.
Courtesy of Kreinik Manufacturing Co., Inc.

Here's Looking At You

Movement and sound. What a marvelous way to keep memories fresh - on videotape! The tape of a special event like a wedding or anniversary deserves a special box to keep it safe and display it proudly.

Assemble

✦ Purchased fabric-covered box
✦ Hand-dyed bias cut silk ribbon (shown, Artemis Wild Iris and Monet) or purchased flowers and leaves
✦ Photo transfer of vintage postcard, greeting card, or fabric appliqué (available from Pleasant Recollections)
✦ Seed beads (shown, Mill Hill #00128)
✦ Plastic leaf beads
✦ Dimensional paint

How To

1. Use ribbons in colors shown or to match photo transfer. Refer to instructions for making leaves and violets on page 14.
2. Iron photo transfer or fuse fabric appliqué at an angle to front of box.
3. Make three violets and three boat leaves. Monet ribbon has a green edge and a pink edge. Sew leaves so pink is along vein. Sew seed beads at 1/4" intervals along vein.
4. Glue silk flowers, leaves, and plastic leaf beads to box. Refer to photo for position. If using purchased flowers, remove stems first.
5. Add dimensional paint swirls and tendrils and let dry.

What Else

✦ Add charms, beads, buttons, and other dimensional embellishment.
✦ Edge lid of box with ruffle or trim.
✦ Write a message, name, and date inside lid with fine-line permanent marker.
✦ Embellish back of box with photo transfer, writing, or fabric paint.

Wish Tree

Set the elegant wish tree on a small table at a wedding reception or anniversary party. Ask each guest to write something to the guests of honor on cards you provide. Clip each wish to a branch and display the tree for everyone to enjoy. After the party, tuck the cards into a keepsake envelope (another project in this chapter), or use them for memory album pages. The tree can be used again and again. Follow the instructions to make your own wish cards or photocopy and decorate the ones provided.

You can make a tree out of old spools, plain wire, a chunk of wood, and big sturdy clothespins for a family reunion picnic or to sprout reminders and photos on your desk.

Assemble
✦ Large round wooden drapery finial
✦ Wood plaques, half circle and small round
✦ Wood hearts
✦ 16-gauge cloth-wrapped stem wire
✦ Ivory ribbon rosettes and silk rosebuds
✦ Satin leaves
✦ Drill with 5/64" bit
✦ Ranger DecorIt inks - Spring Green, Navy, Gold (or colors desired)
✦ Tan spray paint
✦ Cosmetic sponge wedge
✦ Latex gloves (very important)
✦ Quick grabbing craft glue
✦ Mini clothespins
✦ Wire cutter
✦ Gold and white markers
✦ Black and muted rose paper
✦ Scallop edge scissors

How To
1. Refer to diagram and glue, screw, or nail finial and plaques together.
2. Glue evenly spaced hearts around sides of base. As shown, the project required 13.
3. Cut some wires to shorter lengths. Glue clothespins, clip side up, to wires. Some get one clip at end, others get several spaced at intervals. Lay wires on protected work surface until glue dries.
4. Drill holes in ball of finial. Glue wires securely into holes. Refer to photo.

Wish Cards

5. Take project outdoors. Cover a large area with newspaper. Spray project with tan paint and let dry.
6. Wearing latex gloves (inks are permanent and dry quickly), use cosmetic sponges to dab entire project including wires with Gold ink, then dab areas with Spring Green and Navy. Use leaf dabbed with each color to stamp leaf shapes on base and finial. Some tan will show through. The effect is antique and random, not controlled or planned.
7. Count number of clothespins in project. For each, dab a satin leaf with Gold, and while still wet, with Navy.

8. Glue leaf and rosette to each clothespin. Glue rosebud to some, but not all. Hold in place with masking tape while glue dries.
9. Cut 3" square of acid-free paper for each wish card. Using scallop edge scissors, cut 2" square of black paper and glue small square on large square at an angle. Decorate with gold pen.
Option: Photocopy wish cards on this page and embellish as desired.
10. Have gold and black markers available at party for guests to write wishes.

What Else
✦ Use gold and white for a more traditional wedding look.
✦ Tie a knot in a 5" x 3/4" strip of fabric to decorate each clothespin for a country look.
✦ Use large gold paper clips instead of clothespins.
✦ Find colorful wire and put pompoms on the clips for a birthday wish tree.

Champagne & Caviar

This music box was designed to celebrate the 25th anniversary of Kreinik Manufacturing Co., Inc. Kreinik makes the fabulous metallic threads and ribbons I have used throughout this book and was the first company to hire me when I began my needlework design career.

The stitching looks like champagne bubbles and glistening caviar. The elegant swirls are made with torsade, a twisted metallic cord, and Facets, a metallic braid that looks like tiny mirrored squares. The music box comes with many different songs. Be sure to request one that's just right for the recipient. This heirloom would befit any occasion.

Assemble

✦ Kreinik 1/8" metallic ribbon 005 Black
✦ 24" 4mm Kreinik Torsade, gold
✦ Skein Kreinik Facets, gold
✦ Gold seed and large black bugle beads from Mill Hill
✦ Sewing needle, bead needle
✦ Gold and black sewing thread
✦ Music jewelry box from Sudberry House
✦ Black velvet fabric 8" x 10"
✦ Quilt batting (cut one 4" x 6", two 3" x 5", one 6½" x 8½")
✦ Two each 8" and 10" stretcher bars
✦ Stapler or thumb tacks
✦ Tracing paper, pencil
✦ Craft glue

How To

1. Review French knot instructions on page 16.

2. Attach velvet to stretcher bars to keep it taut while working. Do not use an embroidery hoop - it leaves marks on velvet.

3. Trace diagram. Cut into sections along lines marked "torsade" and use it as a guide as torsade is sewn in place with tiny stitches (gold thread). Let cut ends of torsade extend beyond edge of fabric. Tape ends to prevent unraveling.

4. Add Facets, French knots, and beads (in that order), using diagram for placement.

5. Layer batting, smaller pieces first, on cardboard insert that comes with

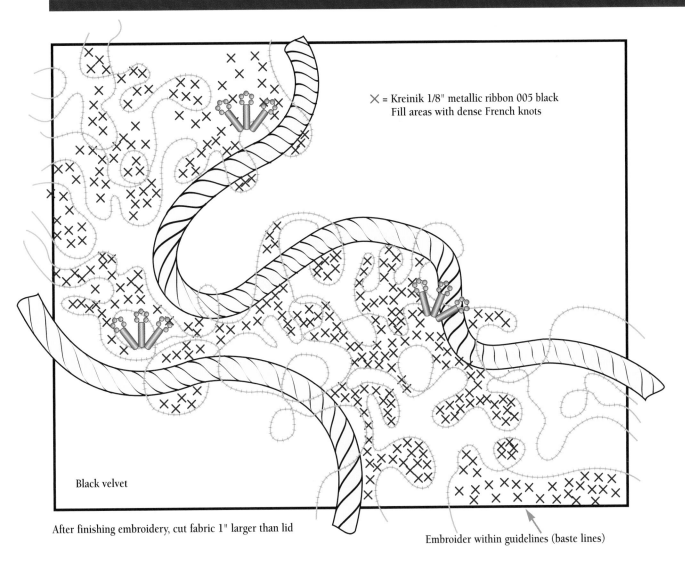

X = Kreinik 1/8" metallic ribbon 005 black
Fill areas with dense French knots

Black velvet

After finishing embroidery, cut fabric 1" larger than lid

Embroider within guidelines (baste lines)

music box. With black sewing thread doubled in needle and a medium length running stitch, gather embroidered velvet over padded cardboard. Tie securely.

6. Glue in place on music box lid. Wrap box tightly in towel and weight with a book to hold padded cardboard in place until glue dries.

What Else

✦ Change the color combination. Use white moiré, metallic ribbon, and beads for a soft, feminine music box. Substitute green marbleized fabric and beads for a woodland music box.

✦ Add buttons, charms, or photo transfers for further embellishment.

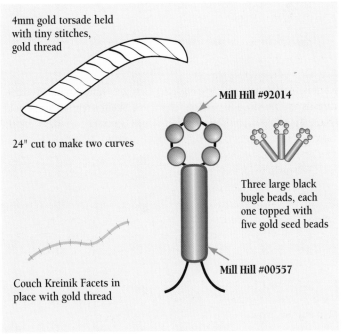

4mm gold torsade held with tiny stitches, gold thread

24" cut to make two curves

Couch Kreinik Facets in place with gold thread

Mill Hill #92014

Three large black bugle beads, each one topped with five gold seed beads

Mill Hill #00557

Chapter Four
Vacation & Travel

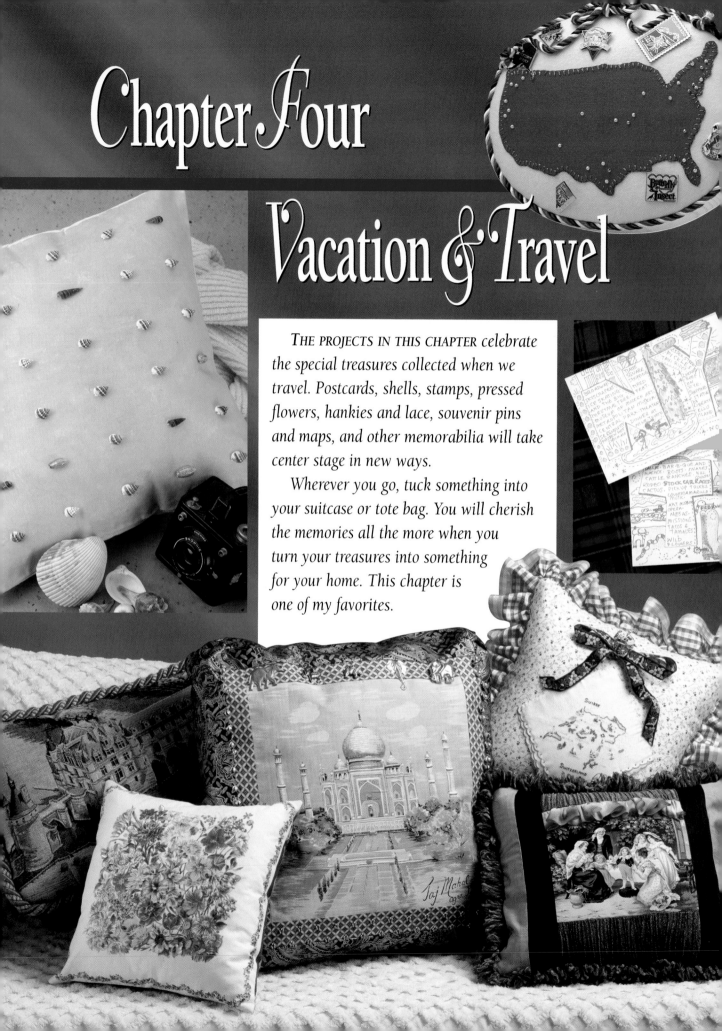

THE PROJECTS IN THIS CHAPTER *celebrate the special treasures collected when we travel. Postcards, shells, stamps, pressed flowers, hankies and lace, souvenir pins and maps, and other memorabilia will take center stage in new ways.*

Wherever you go, tuck something into your suitcase or tote bag. You will cherish the memories all the more when you turn your treasures into something for your home. This chapter is one of my favorites.

Maps For Treasures

The Maps for Treasures wall hanging, pillow sham, and box are made of sturdy wool felt, perfect for pinning and rearranging souvenirs.

My friend Eileen is one of six children. When she was little, her family lived all over the world while her father served in the military. On vacation, each of the children wore a hat covered with pins purchased on trips or brought home as gifts. The wall hanging of Europe features her collection.

My husband collects campaign buttons. His treasures are on the U.S. map pillow. The memory box is mine. I sewed a pearl to each city we've visited and a gold bead to each place where we have lived.

Assemble

✦ Map, enlarged to size for finished project
✦ National Nonwovens' 70% wool felt in colors shown or as desired, additional for back of pillow sham

(amounts determined by size of map and finished project)
✦ Kreinik metallic braid or DMC Medicis wool to edge and decorate maps
✦ Machine embroidery thread
✦ Tracing paper
✦ Bold black marker
✦ Paper-backed fusible webbing
✦ Heavy duty iron-on stabilizer for wall hanging (Crafter's Choice from HTC)
✦ Twisted cord
If making the box, you'll also need:
✦ Large oval moiré-covered box from Sudberry House
✦ Quilt batting
✦ Beads
✦ Fabric glue

How To

1. Enlarge map to size desired (many photocopy centers make copies up to three feet). Pillow sham and oval box require horizontal maps. Wall hanging can be any shape.

2. Simplify map with black marker. Trace and cut out pattern pieces.
3. Iron paper-backed fusible webbing to back of colors used for map (not background). Do not remove paper. Pin patterns to right side of felt and cut out.
4. Arrange map on background felt. Following manufacturer's directions, remove backing paper and fuse in place.
5. Add machine embroidery on map to resemble highways and around it for a decorative border (like pillow sham), edge with blanket stitch using metallic braid (like box), or stitch around map with bright colored wool (like wall hanging).
6. Refer to page 10 for directions on finishing pillows and wall hangings.
7. Complete oval box following manufacturer's directions. Add quilt batting for padded lid. Starting at top center, glue twisted cord around edge. Glue bow over joining point of cord.

What Else

✦ Make a world map for the classroom. Sew a button or charm at every location studied or where students have family and friends.
✦ Use a different print fabric for each state or country. Cover raw edges of fused appliqués with dimensional paint.

Fabric Memorabilia Pillows

Victorian ladies collected picture pillows for their parlors. Proudly displayed on an ornate velvet love seat, the pillows were souvenirs from the World's Fair or a distant destination. Perhaps they were sent by a brother or given by a suitor.

Make your own souvenir pillows from what I lovingly call "fabric memorabilia" - the hankies, fabric pictures, and jacquard tapestries found all over the world in flea markets, tourist kiosks, fabric stores, and elegant boutiques. They are easy to pack, inexpensive, and unbreakable.

I made five different kinds of pillows so you can decide which style suits what you have collected. Refer to page 10 for instructions on how to finish pillows.

Assemble
✦ Fabric memorabilia
✦ Trim, piping, fringe, beads, charms, embellishments
✦ Pillow insert
✦ Backing fabric

How To
1. When your fabric looks good with just a hint of embellishment. Fuse fine, sheer fabrics like the handkerchief in the English Garden pillow to a lightweight stabilizer. Sew embellishments that match the scale of the print. I chose tiny Mill Hill glass animals, bugs, and leaves and hid them between the flowers to discover close up. The pillow is small, so the handkerchief forms the entire front.

2. When your fabric is small or delicate and needs to be visually anchored by other elements. The Map of Switzerland pillow has a hankie sewn just below center so there is room for a generous bow and souvenir pin at the top. The hankie is folded, letting all of the corners show and acknowledging what it is. I added tiny seed beads near the scalloped edges. The print fabric enhances but doesn't overpower the hankie. The souvenir pin can be removed if I want to wear it on a jacket or hat.

3. When your fabric is bold and pictorial, add a wide border, stronger prints, and lots of dimensional embellishment. The Taj Mahal pillow has a painted handkerchief fused to a lightweight stabilizer, centered between

Indian-inspired fabric bands. Elephant charms collected on various trips are spaced across the top to leave room for more. Dance bells tinkle at the sides so the pillow sounds like India too. Since Indian textiles are heavily embellished, there are beads in the fabric band at the bottom as well. The corners of the pillow are gathered for a lush effect. The pillow is 20" square.

4. **When you want your pillow to look like it's from another era,** use fine silk or velvet in muted colors and splurge on fringe or tassels. The French Ribbon pillow shows off a silk ribbon brocade picture panel. I surrounded it with crumpled metallic fabric and soft green moiré to feel like France in the 1800s. Sew a hand-dyed silk ribbon ruffle into the seam allowance when adding a fabric strip at the top and the picture panel becomes a stage.

5. **When the fabric panel is firm, large, and needs no embellishment,** frame it with twisted-cord piping. The French Chateau pillow is a souvenir tapestry made into a simple knife edge pillow. Tapestry panels are available at tourist spots from the Grand Canyon to the Loire Valley. If I ever go to Graceland, I'm going to add an Elvis pillow to my collection.

What Else

✦ Instead of a hankie or tapestry, make a postcard or photograph into an iron-on transfer.

✦ Add fabric strip borders as if you were making a square pillow. Sew the squares together for a wall hanging or add batting for a quilt.

✦ Frame the panel like the patchwork heart on page 28.

✦ Decorate pillows as a family project, choosing and collecting items together.

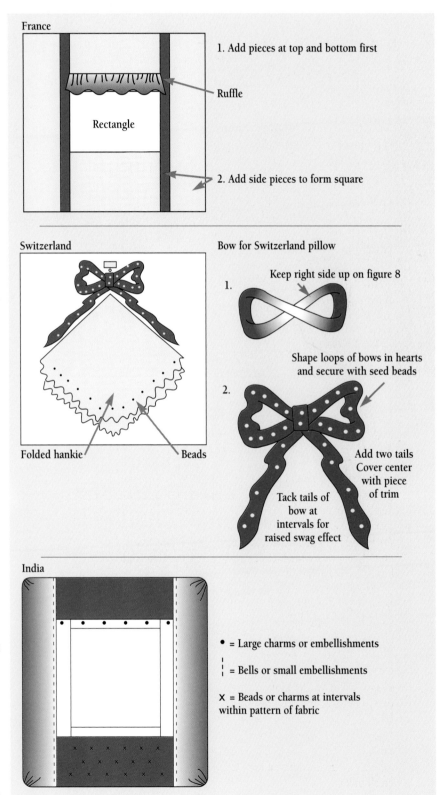

France

1. Add pieces at top and bottom first

Ruffle

Rectangle

2. Add side pieces to form square

Switzerland

Folded hankie

Beads

Bow for Switzerland pillow

Keep right side up on figure 8

1.

Shape loops of bows in hearts and secure with seed beads

2.

Add two tails
Cover center with piece of trim

Tack tails of bow at intervals for raised swag effect

India

• = Large charms or embellishments

┊ = Bells or small embellishments

x = Beads or charms at intervals within pattern of fabric

Nature Lover's Notebook

Cover a binder with a fabric collage and add buttons that a nature lover would enjoy. Use as a journal for birdwatching or fill the pages with pressed botanicals. The center panel is made of folded fabrics sewn or glued in place one at a time, starting in the middle.

Assemble

✦ Three-ring binder
✦ Canvas and natural-color print fabric scraps (see Diagram C for measurements)
✦ Acorn, bird, tree buttons (all from JHB International) or other nature theme buttons
✦ Fabric glue (optional)
✦ Sewing thread to match canvas

How To

1. Cut, fold, and sew or glue fabric pieces following Diagram B to create center medallion. If gluing on buttons, remove shanks.
2. Measure your notebook. The size of spine determines how much additional fabric you have to sew on. See Diagram C for measurements.
3. Turn short ends to wrong side 1/2" and machine hem. Turn under long sides at fold line 1. Fold under again at fold line 2. Tack at edge. Insert binder.
4. Sew or glue buttons to medallion.

What Else

✦ Collect buttons as souvenirs and add them to the cover.
✦ Choose textured, earth-toned, or botanical print fabrics instead of canvas.
✦ Use floral print fabrics with butterfly, bee, and flower buttons.
✦ Make the medallion into a pillow or appliqué it to the front of a canvas tote.

8" square muslin

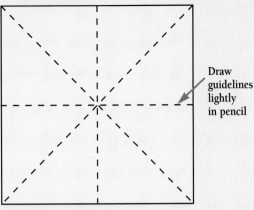

Draw guidelines lightly in pencil

Diagram A

1. Build pattern from the center, following Diagram B
2. Add fabric strips to complete notebook cover
3. Glue buttons in place

Note: Raw edges are covered by each piece added. Refer to photo.

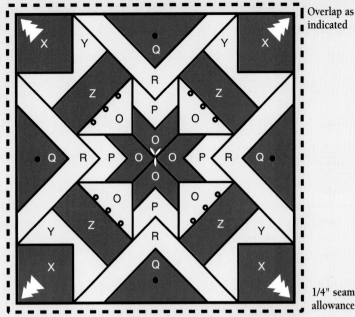

Overlap as indicated

1/4" seam allowance

Diagram B

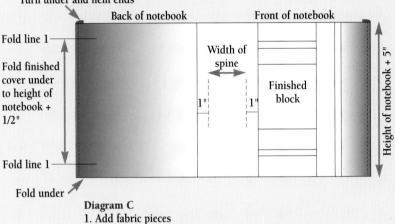

Turn under and hem ends

Back of notebook

Front of notebook

Fold line 1

Fold finished cover under to height of notebook + 1/2"

Width of spine

Finished block

1"   1"

Height of notebook + 5"

Fold line 1

Fold under

Diagram C

1. Add fabric pieces
2. Hem short ends
3. Fold under long sides

Fold line 2

Diagram D

1. Fold under short ends
2. Sew with blind stitches
3. Insert notebook

⌀ Acorn

● Barbie button

● Bird

🌲 Tree

Fold corners down

Center four O units with folded side up. All other pointed units have folded sides facing down.

Trim block to 8" (muslin piece) when layers are completed

1. Make eight off-white units (O), four off-white print units (P), four rust/orange solid color units (Q)
2. Make four rust print units as above, starting with 5" squares (R)
3. Fold four off-white print 4" squares in half (Z)
4. Fold four dark rust solid color 4" squares in half (Y)
5. Fold four tan solid squares in half twice for corner units (X)

On The Road Postcards

Remember those souvenir postcards from the 1940s and '50s with big lettering and hundreds of little drawings all over them? Tuck some colored pencils or markers and a packet of blank postcards into your purse and have fun doodling your way from place to place when you travel. Children will enjoy sharing this project.

Assemble

✦ Colored pencils or markers
✦ Blank postcards or card stock cut to postcard size
✦ Pencil sharpener
✦ Magnets (optional)
✦ Xyron laminating machine or film

How To

1. Practice on scrap paper if you want. Outline big, chunky letters to spell name of place you are visiting. I used two-letter postal abbreviations.
2. Doodle things that you see. This isn't drawing class, this is **doodling**, so be playful and goofy.
3. Write words and sentence fragments. Add squiggles and dots and fill space with colorful designs.
4. Send some to friends and some to yourself.

What Else

✦ When you get home, laminate some of the cards and make jumbo refrigerator magnets.
✦ Put the postcards in memory albums along with photos from the trip.
✦ Make postcards when you're not on a trip. Send them for no reason. Remember, a hundred years from now, they're going to be the vintage treasures someone will discover. E-mail disappears into the air.

Postcard Mosaics

This project is a favorite with all of my friends. People who've never tried a craft of any kind want to make one. Craft enthusiasts immediately see ways to use the technique for other projects.

Assemble
✦ Postcards or photographs
✦ Table with raised edge
✦ Double-faced adhesive sheets from ThermOWeb (enough to cover tabletop)
✦ Gold embossing powder (or color desired)
✦ Heat tool
✦ Craft knife and cutting mat
✦ Metal straight edge (optional)
✦ EnviroTex Lite (pour-on coating, amount determined by size of table)

How To
Reminder: Images get bigger when they are cut apart and spaced to look like mosaics.

1. Cover top of table with double-faced adhesive sheet and remove protective paper so whole area is sticky.

2. Lay postcards or photos, one at a time, on cutting mat. Cut them into small pieces to use as mosaic "tiles." They do not need to be perfect squares - some should be slightly angled to look broken. Cut some smaller than others.

3. Space tiles on sticky adhesive, leaving 1/4" to 3/8" between them as "grout" lines. Refer to photo.

4. Omit any areas of postcard or photo that you don't like. Angle postcards or keep them lined up in more formal grid if you prefer.

5. Cover eraser end of a pencil with fabric so it won't scratch cards and use it to gently burnish each tile in place. Be careful not to touch exposed adhesive between tiles.

6. Sprinkle embossing powder over table. Shake excess off onto newspaper and put it back in jar for another project. If just a bit sticks to tiles, they will look gilded, but too much excess on tiles will cover pictures.

7. Use heat tool to emboss grout areas. Do not over-heat as adhesive might curl.

8. Follow manufacturer's instructions for EnviroTex Lite to seal top of table. Dry thoroughly and apply second or third layer if desired (I used three coats).

What Else
✦ Add low-profile buttons, pressed flowers, or other memorabilia. You will need three to five thin layers of EnviroTex Lite to cover these items.
✦ Cut postcards into strips instead of squares.
✦ Make mosaic tiles from color copies of children's drawings.
✦ Create a theater lover's keepsake table with tickets and playbills cut into tiles.

Seashell Pillow

For many years, I kept all the shells I collected in a basket. The idea for this pillow popped into my head when I decided they'd look better spread out in some way. The texture of canvas fabric looks and feels like sand, and the glitter in the fabric paint reminds me of sun sparkling on water. Choose colors to go with your décor.

If you can't get to the beach or you want exotic shapes and shells dyed in different colors, see the Resource Guide for a mail order source and buy some.

Assemble

✦ Small shells
✦ Two squares natural canvas fabric 1" larger than size of finished pillow plus extra canvas to practice painting
✦ Pillow insert
✦ Sewing thread to match canvas
✦ Iridescent fabric paint (I mixed lime and yellow)
✦ Fabric glue
✦ Cosmetic sponge wedge or wide brush

How To

1. Experiment with paint on scrap of fabric.
2. Lay canvas squares on protected work surface. Squeeze paint on plate. Using cosmetic sponge or paint brush, lightly cover surface of canvas with paint.
3. After paint dries, repeat for areas that need more and dry again.
4. Arrange shells in rows as shown or in any pattern you like. Glue them in position with fabric glue and let dry.
5. Refer to page 10 for directions on sewing a pillow.

What Else

✦ Make a wall hanging instead of a pillow.
✦ Paint a canvas apron and glue shells to the pocket or hem.
✦ Create a row of pillows, each one with a different kind of shell.
✦ Stencil shapes or pictures on the canvas and decorate with shells.

Stamp A Memory

Postage stamps are miniature works of art, taking us around the world to exotic locations. Canceled stamps make wonderful bits of color to use for collage.

Assemble

✦ Canceled stamps

Boxes and Basket:

✦ Paper or wood box or basket
✦ Beads, buttons, charms, optional decorations
✦ Matte finish acrylic medium or Liquid Laminate
✦ Paint brush

Place Mats:

✦ 11" x 17" white paper
✦ Xyron machine, 2-sided laminate cartridge
✦ Craft glue

How To

Boxes and Basket

1. Carefully peel canceled stamps from envelopes by tearing the paper a little at a time from each edge.
2. Cover lid, sides, and inside of box or basket with stamps. Use either acrylic medium or Liquid Laminate to glue stamps to surfaces. When dry, add second coat for durability. Large box was brushed with acrylic medium tinted with brown acrylic paint for antique effect.
3. Sew small shell button topped with bead to lid of box or side of basket as decoration.

Place Mats

1. For each mat, glue canceled stamps to 11" x 17" piece of white paper.
2. Laminate on Xyron machine or have professionally laminated.

What Else

✦ Make iron-on transfers and decorate napkins to match.
✦ Instead of white paper, use fabric or a map as the place mat background.
✦ Cover the entire mat with stamps, overlapping like on the boxes so no background shows.

Chapter Five

Family Celebrations, Storytelling & Memories

MY DEFINITION OF FAMILY is broad. It includes people I'm related to by blood and marriage and the friends who have become like sisters. It also includes my goddaughter and the children who have adopted me into their circles, former students whose lives remain meshed with mine, and my family of craft and needlework friends.

The projects in this chapter celebrate the connections and links we make and share through stories and sayings, teaching and learning, giving and receiving, cooking and feasting.

My special favorites are the sewing boxes and the Story Starter quilts and pillow. Learning to sew was a high point of my childhood - fabric and threads remain my prized possessions. My family told stories instead of watching television. I remember prompting my mother and father to repeat the "best" stories by saying the first line and waiting for them to fill in the rest.

Story Necklace

For a time, Orange Potter, Esq., the photographer/illustrator, lived by the beach in Maine. During his daily walks, he searched for perfect shells that were all the same size. Then, while he was "warming up" his drawing hand to work on a book called *Charles, The Cardboard Turtle* (sadly, not yet published), he painted a story about a mermaid on the shells, creating a necklace he gave to his favorite professor on Valentine's Day.

I am that teacher and the necklace is a gift I will treasure all my life. I cannot give directions, because there are none. I show it to you with the hope that it will inspire you to write a story for someone you care about and spend the time to make it special.

Look for something unusual on which to write or paint. Shells or wooden beads for a necklace, blocks of wood or rocks and pebbles, fabric pieces or found objects, all make interesting choices.

Words Of Wisdom Necklace

Before computers spit out vinyl wristbands for new babies, infants wore bracelets with their names spelled out in alphabet beads surrounded by pink or blue beads tied on a string. The beads still exist, sold in bags at craft stores. I thought they'd be perfect for making jewelry that carried words of wisdom - a favorite saying, a Bible verse, or something your parents, grandparents, or favorite teacher always said.

Assemble
✦ Jewelry pliers
✦ Alphabet beads from Darice
✦ Additional beads in color(s) and size(s) desired
✦ Jewelry findings: one eye pin per letter or bead; chain the length desired; jump rings
✦ Clasp (optional)
✦ Bead design board (optional)

How To
1. Arrange alphabet, spacer beads, and chain on bead design board (tray with ridges to keep beads from rolling off).
2. Use jewelry pliers to make link with each letter or bead (see diagram).
3. Connect links and chain. For bracelets or necklaces that won't slip over your head, add clasp at midpoint of chain.

What Else
✦ Make a funky necklace with the punch line of a favorite joke.
✦ Spell out the names of your children and grandchildren, separated by birthstone-colored beads.
✦ Repeat your initials over and over.
✦ Spell out a song, birthday greeting, or other message.
✦ Use larger scale beads (alphabet beads come in many sizes) and make a banner for the mantel, classroom, or office.

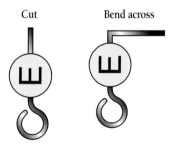

Cut   Bend across

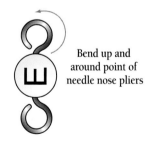

Bend up and around point of needle nose pliers

Link together

Space between words with plain beads

Story Starter Quilts & Pillow

It's bedtime. A beloved child is tucked under a soft warm quilt. It's story time. A grandchild props her head against a big floppy pillow. The stories start like this:

Once upon a time… When I was a little girl, I lived across the sea… Your grandfather always told me…

Make that special child a comforter or pillow from prequilted fabric covered with the "opening lines" of your favorite stories, hopes, and dreams. Or let her/him write his own Story Starters. I made the pillow for my new neighbor, Daniel David, whose parents crossed the world to adopt him in Russia.

Assemble
Pillow is 20" square, quilts are 40" x 65"
✦ Prequilted wavy line muslin from The Warm Co.
✦ Print fabric for ruffle: 6" strip, three times outside measurement of quilt or pillow (optional)
✦ Backing fabric for ruffled quilt (optional)
✦ Five or more colors of embroidery floss for hem of plain quilt

✦ Fabric markers in black or colors desired
✦ Buttons, charms, or other embellishments

How To
Quilt and Pillow
1. Distress fabric to make it look loved and worn. Throw it in washing machine set on hot wash and cold rinse. Machine dry on high. It will shrink and rumple. Do not iron.
2. Practice writing on paper to see how long phrases will be and decide on lettering style.
Quilt
1. Trace part of saucer to round corners of quilt rectangle. For ruffled version, attach ruffle and backing fabric as if you were making a table runner (see page 10).
2. Tie with embroidery floss, hand or machine tack with sewing thread at intervals to hold backing fabric in place. For plain version, turn raw edge to front 1/4", repeat, easing at curves, and hem in place with large straight stitches using six strands of embroidery floss. Change colors at

frequent but random intervals.
3. Write on quilt between all quilting lines, every other line, or as desired. Use fine line marker, bold marker, one color, or many colors.
4. Draw hearts and pictures, sew on buttons or charms (not for infants who might choke), and embellish as desired.
Pillow
1. Cut pillow front and back from prewashed quilted fabric.
2. Decorate front only, or both sides.
3. Finish pillow as shown or with ruffle (see page 10).

What Else
✦ Let each member of the family write the first line of his/her favorite story.
✦ Make a quilt as a class project. Have each person make up a story or copy the first line from a favorite book.
✦ Machine or hand quilt your own fabric with a different pattern (straight lines, zigzags, swirls, boxes, or free motion curves). Use a specialty thread like metallic or rayon. Instead of straight stitches, quilt with a decorative embroidery stitch.

Cherished Recipes: Pockets & Cards

Cinnamon makes me think of my grandmothers. Grandma Rose made yeasty and voluptuous cinnamon rolls. Grandma Tina made soft cookies sprinkled with the tiniest hint of spice. Their recipes were never written down. Both cooked from feel. I would give anything to have their recipes to duplicate for my friends and family, but they are lost forever.

I designed these recipe pockets as a way to preserve the memories that come from our kitchens. I chose vintage apron fabrics for a nostalgic look.

The pockets fit standard 3" x 5" and 4" x 6" cards. The cards provided are for you to photocopy and decorate with colored pencils, markers, and stickers. Tell the copy center you have the author's permission to make as many as you want for your own use.

Assemble
✦ Fabric and matching sewing thread
✦ Buttons, charms, ball fringe, and other embellishments
✦ Twisted or rattail cord, ribbon, thin braid

How To
1. Trace pattern. Pin pattern to fabric and cut two pieces for each pocket.
2. With right sides of fabric together, sew around sides and bottom point. Pattern includes 1/4" seam allowance.
3. Clip corners and turn right side out. Turn top edge under 1/4", then again at hem line. Machine, hand stitch, or fuse hem.
4. Add embellishments as shown or as desired. Sew on a hanging loop at sides or center.

What Else

✦ Hang recipe pockets on a clothes-line or tree branch at a family reunion and ask everyone to bring a card to tuck inside. Enlarge the pocket size if you have a big family!

✦ Take one with you when you take homemade goodies to a party.
✦ Double or triple the pocket size and tuck a cookbook inside.
✦ Write names, dates, or messages on the fabric in permanent marker.

✦ Use specialty prints for holidays. At Christmas add a tassel to the bottom to use pockets for ornaments. At Easter tuck a decorated egg inside along with the recipe. For Valentine's Day, candy hearts would be fun.

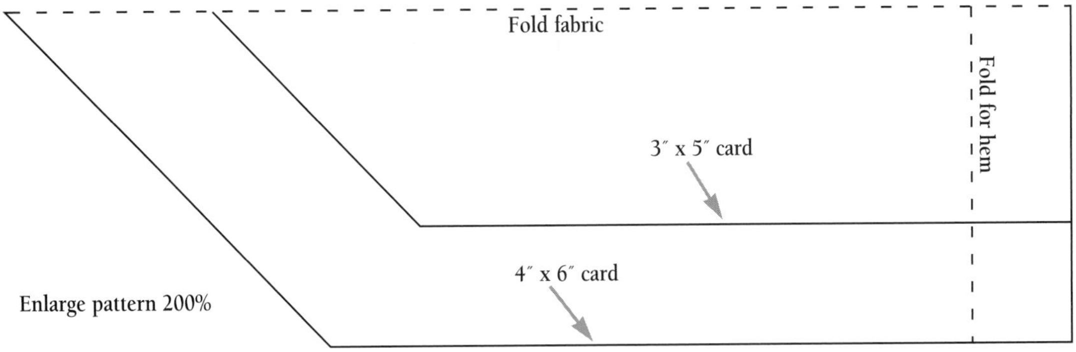

From My Kitchen to Yours

Recipe: From:

From My Kitchen to Yours

Recipe: From:

Fold fabric

Fold for hem

3″ x 5″ card

4″ x 6″ card

Enlarge pattern 200%

Learning To Sew

Whether you take a class at age fifty or learn to sew as a small child, I'm sure your sewing box will become your constant companion and cherished possession. Make one for someone you love or for yourself. The ribbon embroidery box uses only two easy stitches. The lace and button collage is a no-sew quickie project. The spool-top boxes on page 58 are needlepoint on rigid canvas.

Button & Lace Collage Basket

Assemble
✦ Muslin-covered sewing box (shown, St. Jane Collection from Dritz)
✦ Vintage or tea-dyed lace, braid, and trims
✦ Larger piece vintage cutwork, doily, or tea-dyed fabric to fit lid (shown, tea-dyed bread tray liner)
✦ Buttons (with shanks removed) and charms
✦ Fabric and jewelry glue

How To
1. Center cutwork or doily on lid. Arrange lace, trims, and braids around borders of lid and bottom of basket. Use more than one width for contrast. Pin to hold while you work. Glue in place with fabric glue, turning cut ends under.
2. Arrange buttons and charms. Glue in place with jewelry glue.

What Else
✦ Use bright colorful new embellishments instead of muted vintage pieces.
✦ Decorate a fabric-covered hatbox.

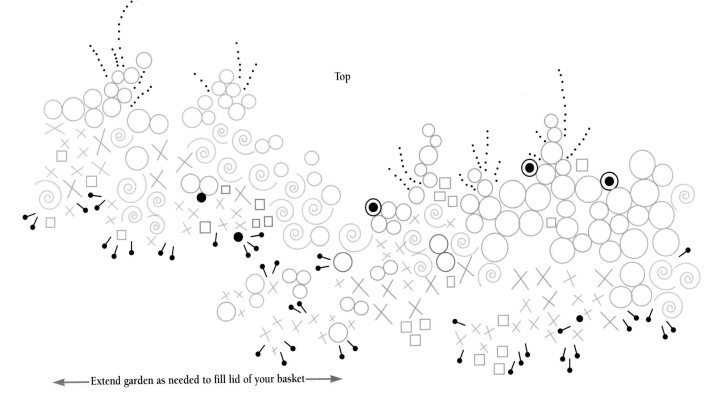

Top

← Extend garden as needed to fill lid of your basket →

Ribbon Embroidery Basket

Assemble

✦ Basket with flat top
✦ Acid-free board to cover top
✦ Five pieces quilt batting to cover cardboard
✦ Velvet or other heavy fabric 2" bigger than basket top
✦ 4mm, 7mm, and 13mm variegated and solid color silk ribbon from Bucilla
✦ Seed beads and glass treasures in colors listed or as desired (shown, Mill Hill)
✦ Chenille needle, bead needle
✦ Thread to match background fabric
✦ Craft glue

How To

1. Cut cardboard to fit top of basket. Using cardboard as a template, baste or pin a guideline on fabric for embroidery area.
2. Review directions for French knots and Japanese ribbon stitch on page 16.
3. Choose ribbon colors and fabric to match fabric and basket or follow chart.
4. Extend or shorten "garden" to fit fabric. Stitch French knot flower clusters and add Japanese ribbon stitch leaves between and around flowers. Don't try to duplicate design exactly.
5. Sew seed beads at intervals in rows of four or five. Add small glass flowers among French knots to add sparkle. Sew seed bead to center of each 13mm French knot flower.
6. Cut four pieces of batting same size as cardboard. Cut one piece 2" larger. Layer and lightly glue batting pieces to each other and to cardboard, largest piece on top.
7. Lay embroidered garden over batting. Stitch sewing thread doubled in needle with a running stitch through fabric and batting 1/2" from edge. Gather to finish padded lid. Cut away excess batting and fabric to eliminate bulk.
8. Glue to basket.

What Else

✦ Instead of a basket, embroider a lid for an oval moiré box like the one on page 41.

	Japanese ribbon stitch

¡ Japanese ribbon stitch
4mm three or four assorted greens (choose greens that go with background fabric). As shown, 638 Parrot, 509 Olive, 561 Pale Grass.

Bucilla Variegated Silk Ribbon as listed or in colors desired

French knots

☐ 7mm 7105 Daffodil

✕ 13mm 1314 Terra Cotta

◯ 7mm 7108 Tropical Brights

◯ 13mm 1307 Lavender & Lace

✕ 7mm 1307 Lavender & Lace

◎ 13mm 1308 Ice Cream

◉ Mill Hill Glass Treasures: flowers

● Mill Hill Glass Treasures: green crystals

⋰ Mill Hill seed beads

Needlepoint Spool Box

Assemble
✦ 6-strand embroidery floss as listed or in alternative colors
✦ Kreinik 1/16" metallic ribbon and braid as listed or color of choice
✦ 14-count plastic canvas
✦ Tapestry needle
✦ Synthetic suede or felt, fabric scraps, and batting for finishing
✦ Craft glue
✦ Card stock cut to dimensions on diagram
✦ Twisted cord or narrow trim

How To
1. Refer to basic needlepoint instructions on page 12. Variegated embroidery floss is used for each spool of thread. Use colors as listed for black background box or choose your favorite colors to create different combination as I did on teal version. To design your own, choose colors for elements - border (dark color), spool (silver or brown work well), threads (different variegated flosses), and inner border (repeat variegated flosses combined with spool color).

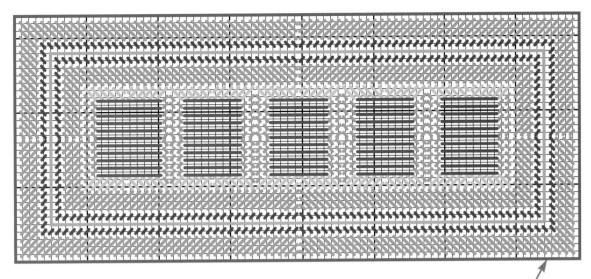

Base - Stitch outer border only and overcast edges like lid

Overcast edges

	Colorway I Brights	Colorway II Muted
Threads on spools, left to right *Long stitches (2 layers if needed for coverage)*	#1 A 1213 Creme de menthe #2 A 1208 Grape #3 A 1219 Citrus #4 A 1210 Royal Spectrum #5 A 1204 Cherry Supreme	#1 NN 166 Pampas Grass #2 NN 148 Mountain Laurel #3 NN 134 Caribbean Skies #4 NN 107 Dreamscape #5 NN 149 Hydrangea
Spool	K A 001 Silver	A 899 Tan
Couched line	A 1213 held by K 001 Silver	NN 107 held by A 899
Double border	outer left 1/2 A 1219, inner left 1/2 A 1210 outer right 1/2 A 1208, inner right 1/2 A 1204	
Background 2 skeins Colorway I A 403 Black; Border 2 skeins Colorway II A 851 Dusty Blue		

Inner border

Couch with upright stitches every other hole, diagonal at corners

A = Anchor 6-strand floss, **NN** = Needle Necessities over-dyed floss, **K** = Kreinik #16 med braid
Overcast edges Kreinik 1/16" metallic ribbon - Colorway I #005 Black, Colorway II #018 Navy

2. Following chart, stitch lid and base of box. Cut out pieces, leaving one row of exposed plastic on all sides. Overcast edges with metallic ribbon held at an angle. Stitch three times at corners for good coverage.
3. Glue synthetic suede to bottom of base. Cut batting to pad outside of each cardboard side piece. Cover batting with fabric, wrapping to back and gluing excess to wrong side. Cover inside of pieces with fabric or synthetic suede. Glue four sides to each other and to base. Hold sides together with tape while glue dries.

4. Line lid with synthetic suede. Cut cardboard rectangle 1/2" smaller than lid. Pad it with batting and cover with fabric. Glue under lid for pincushion.
5. Glue twisted cord and bow around bottom rim.

What Else
✦ Stitch several rows of spools for a larger box. Adjust side and bottom pieces to match.
✦ For a quick and easy alternative, stitch only the lid. Glue it to the top of a plastic box with compartments or the top of a fabric-covered box.

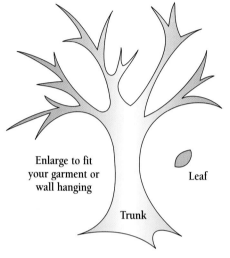

Enlarge to fit your garment or wall hanging

Leaf

Trunk

Family Tree

An exquisite family tree drawn in pen and ink hung in my grandmother's front hall. It had little ovals on the branches holding photographs of family members. It was framed and completed long before I was born. I thought this book should include family tree projects that could be expanded, more "leaves" added with new marriages and babies. One is on a big kitchen towel, another on a T-shirt.

Assemble
✦ Towel (from Wimpole Street Creations), fabric, or garment
✦ Fabric for leaves and trunk
✦ Fabric glue or paper-backed fusible webbing
✦ Fabric markers or dimensional fabric paint
✦ Machine or hand embroidery thread
✦ Iron

How To
No-Sew Version (shown on T-shirt)
1. Start with shirt, banner, towel, or sheet for background. Or fold or glue hems on sides of piece of fabric.
2. Enlarge leaf and trunk patterns to right size for background. Trace around them on paper side of fusible webbing (one leaf per person). Fuse webbing to back of trunk and leaf fabrics.
3. Cut out pieces. Remove paper backing. Fuse trunk and leaves on background.
4. Write names on leaves using fabric marker or dimensional paint. Write name, date or message across bottom.
Sewn Version (shown on towel)
1. Repeat process above, but add machine embroidery to edges of trunk and leaves.
2. Names and dates can be machine embroidered on a programmable sewing machine.

What Else
✦ Prepare trunk and leaves before guests arrive. Together decorate and attach leaves to the tree. Display the banner at family gatherings.
✦ Make dimensional leaves with double layers of fabric. Attach one end of leaf to branch.
✦ Create an heirloom quilt with hand or machine appliqué, embroidery, batting, backing fabric, and then hand or machine quilting. A perfect wedding gift, leaves can be added as the family grows.
✦ Make a tree for a group other than family, like the "Class of…" version shown.
✦ Create a small colorful tree and have multiple copies made to give each family member, or get color iron-on transfers and make a T-shirt or tote bag for each person.

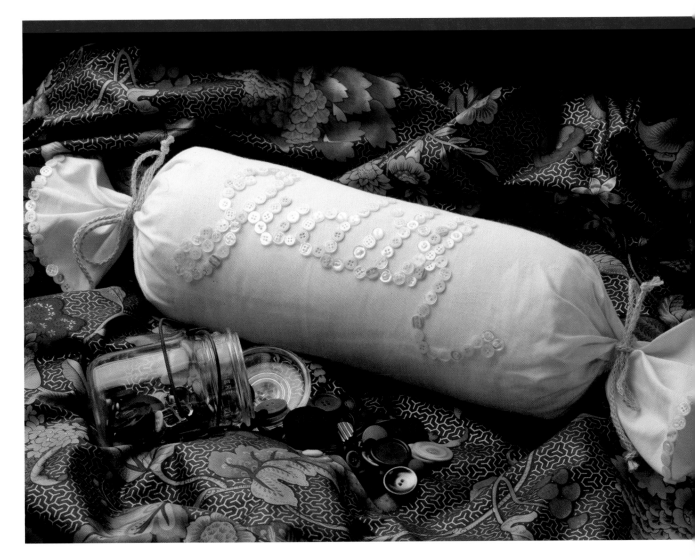

Button Jar Autograph Pillow

This may be the easiest project in the whole book. If you don't have a collection of buttons to use, buy them by the bag. My six-letter name takes about three cups of buttons. I glued the buttons on. If yours are valuable or sentimental, take a little more time and sew them in place.

Assemble
+ Tracing paper
+ Purchased pillow cover
+ Pillow insert
+ Buttons
+ Fabric glue or needle and thread
+ Disappearing ink fabric marker

How To
1. Practice writing your autograph large enough to fill front of pillow until you like the look. Arrange buttons on letters. They can overlap in a random casual way or be in neat rows. The letters are easiest to read if buttons are all one color, but mix colors if you prefer.
2. Draw the autograph on fabric using disappearing ink marker.
3. Glue or sew buttons in place.
4. Add more buttons to hems of a tied bolster pillow as shown.

What Else
+ Make pillows or quilt blocks using children's signatures for an anniversary celebration. Give them to the honored parents or grandparents.
+ Surprise a friend. Enlarge his/her signature on a copy machine.
+ Spell a word (Love, Peace, Hope, Noel) instead of a name.
+ Use beads, ribbon flowers, or tiny bows instead of buttons.

Chapter Six

Holidays

MY FAVORITE HOLIDAY? If you ask me in February, it's Valentine's Day. If you ask me in October, it's Halloween. If you ask me in December… I like the fact that there's an occasion for decorations and celebrations year round.

The projects in this chapter span the seasons. Designated for one holiday or another, many of them would be great at other times. For example, the photo hearts make excellent Valentines and Christmas tree ornaments. For Easter or for a christening, just change the colors - hearts are universal. The button and lace ornaments could become brooches, earrings, or magnets. The foundation-pieced tree doesn't have to be for Christmas, just leave off the holiday decorations.

The memories you create by hand crafting gifts and decorations for holidays are some of the most powerful of all. Happy Easter, Merry Christmas, Happy Mother's Day, Happy Father's Day, Happy Chanukah, Happy Valentine's Day, Happy Halloween! Have a wonderful, creative year.

Photo Hearts

At Valentine's Day, to hang on the Christmas tree, or to send a special "I love you" message, these hearts are fast and easy to make. The texture is a simple stamped and embossed technique.

Assemble

✦ White and gold card stock
✦ Colorbox ink pads: gold, turquoise, black (from Clearsnap)
✦ Gold embossing powder
✦ Heat tool
✦ Scissors or craft knife
✦ Rotary cutter with deckle blade from Fiskars
✦ 12" fine cord or ribbon
✦ 1/16" hole punch from McGill Creativity
✦ Wire
✦ 3"-4" piece of Magic Stamp (PenScore) foam block from Clearsnap
✦ Three 3D-O's adhesive dots from Scratch Art
✦ Acid-free glue or double-faced tape

How To

1. Trace and cut patterns. Use templates to draw shapes on back of card stock.

2. Cut largest heart from gold card stock using deckle edge rotary cutter. Cut medium heart from white stock. Use smallest heart to crop picture.

3. Use ink pads to lightly brush medium heart with gold, turquoise, and black ink at random to coat surface (all three or choose your favorites). Let ink dry.

4. Following manufacturer's directions, heat moldable foam block and press crumpled wire into it to create a textured rubber stamp. See mats and cards in Chapter 10 for more examples of this technique.

5. Stamp medium heart with textured block using gold ink. Sprinkle with gold embossing powder, brush off excess, and use heat tool to emboss texture.

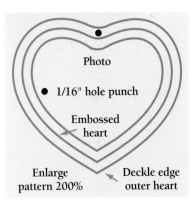

6. Center photo and glue or tape on medium heart. For dimension, add three 3D-O's to back of photo heart. Center on deckle-edge heart.

7. Punch tiny hole at top of gold heart. Thread ribbon or cord through hole to make hanging loop.

What Else

✦ Start with three sizes of a different shape like a square, diamond, or simple flower.
✦ Use lace, a basket, or other texture instead of wire.

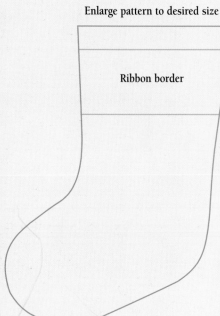

Enlarge pattern to desired size

Ribbon border

Use 1/2" seam allowance for 15" stocking

His Old Shirt Christmas Stockings

Don't discard well- or never-worn shirts. Turn them into dynamite Christmas stockings. One pattern, lots of options. Shown at 15", you can make other sizes too.

Assemble

✦ Two 12" x 16" rectangles cut from shirt or shirt fabrics (larger or smaller if pattern size is changed)

✦ Two 12" x 16" pieces lining fabric (as above)

✦ For plaid flannel stocking: 8" pieces wide tapestry trim, rickrack, and gros-grain ribbon

✦ For patchwork-look stocking: 3/8" red buttons (number depends on fabric) and porcelain tree buttons from Mill Hill

✦ Sewing thread to match

✦ Fabric glue or fusible tape (optional)

How To

1. Enlarge pattern. Cut two stocking and two lining pieces from shirts.

2. For front of striped shirt stocking, cut to include button placket. Sew, glue, or fuse it closed. Cut pocket from shirt front and add it to toe. Baste or pin collar points to top edge.

3. For front of plaid flannel stocking, measure 1½" from top edge and sew, glue, or fuse trims across stocking (shown, 2"-wide tapestry ribbon bordered on both sides by 1/2" gros-grain ribbon and edged with tiny rick-rack hidden halfway under grosgrain).

4. For front of patchwork-look stock-ing, sew red buttons at intervals where fabric looks like attached patches. Sew porcelain tree buttons to three or more solid squares.

5. For all three, make a hanging loop from fabric strip 4" x 8" strip of fabric. Fold long sides under 1", fold in half (raw edges inside), and topstitch. Or use twisted cord, ribbon, or braid.

6. With right sides together and 1/2" seam allowance, sew around foot of stocking.

7. Repeat with lining, leaving a 5"

opening on one side for turning.

8. Trim seam allowance to 1/4" and clip curves. Turn stocking right side out.

9. Fold hanging loop in half. Pin it to side of stocking. Cut ends in seam allowance.

10. Put stocking inside lining (which remains inside out). Pin or baste around top edge.

11. Sew lining and stocking together. Turn right side out through opening in lining. Close opening with small stitches. Push lining into toe of stock-ing.

12. Press top edge, easing lining into stocking so it doesn't show.

What Else

✦ Reduce the size of the stocking and make an ornament.

✦ Cut random shapes from shirts and make a crazy patchwork fabric.

✦ Monogram the shirt pocket using festive green and red machine embroi-dery.

Buttons & Lace

A good way to show off special buttons is to make them into ornaments. These small-scale treasures can be backed with a pin or turned into clip-back earrings. Valuable buttons should be sewn, not glued.

Assemble
✦ Buttons (remove shanks to glue)
✦ Crochet flowers from Wimpole Street Creations (natural shown)
✦ Craft glue or needle and thread
✦ Stiff backing (heavy duty stabilizer/interfacing, crinoline, or lightweight cardboard)
✦ Cord or narrow ribbon

How To
1. Cut backing circle smaller than crochet flower.
2. Arrange buttons on, around, and tucked under edges of flower as shown, or as desired. Glue or sew in place.
3. Add hanging loop at top, or glue to pin back or earring clips.

What Else
✦ Omit backing. Stitch motifs across the cuff of a Christmas stocking, sew onto a sweater, tote bag, or pillow.
✦ Punch 1/8" hole in a circle of white cardboard. Add a greeting to the back, hang from a cord, and use as a gift tag.

Father's Day Game Board

In true pack rat fashion, I've always saved old neckties. The patterns and fabrics are too beautiful to part with and I secretly hoped the ties will come back in style. I finally decided to give my stash of silk a new life by cutting them up into squares for a game board for checkers and chess. Beautiful enough to display in the living room, it's also easy to roll and pack for travel.

Attention beginners and nonquilters! Don't tell Dad how easy it was to make. The secret is a preprinted fusible backing on which you place 2" squares, then iron them into place, turn over the panel, fold, and sew along the printed lines.

Assemble

✦ Silk neckties with two contrasting dominant colors (navy/red, brown/yellow-gold, etc.) or fabric to make thirty-two 2" squares in two colors (sixty-four total)
✦ Quilt-Fuse preprinted fusible quilt piecing material from HTC (as shown, eight 2" squares x eight 2" squares - for larger boards, multiply to enlarge)
✦ Dark sewing thread (or to match fabric)
✦ Backing fabric same size as Quilt-Fuse

How To

1. Cut thirty-two 2" squares in each of two colors. The tip of one necktie will yield three to six squares, depending on width of tie.
2. Arrange squares on textured (fusible) side of Quilt-Fuse, alternating colors. Iron squares in place.
3. Turn over, fold on straight lines, and sew all parallel lines in one direction. Turn and repeat for all parallel lines in second direction, following manufacturer's directions.
4. Back with fabric like a flat wall hanging (see directions on page 10).

What Else

✦ Cut 4" or 8" squares of fabric for a larger size board and adjust the dimensions of Quilt-Fuse accordingly.
✦ Use cotton and make a washable version.
✦ Make fabric yo-yos to use as checkers.
✦ Put a zipper pocket on the back to store checkers or chess pieces for a travel game.

Roses For Mother's Day

Get the effect of decoupage without intricate cutting by using an easy combination of stickers and a brush-on gloss finish. There are so many wonderful stickers available. Choose flowers like the pansies in Chapter 10, teacups, or animals - whatever you think the recipient would like. Make boxes for other occasions too.

Assemble
✦ Paper maché box
✦ Victorian rose stickers (from Sticker Planet) or other stickers
✦ Ranger DecorIt inks - Gold, Spring Green, Navy and Cranberry as shown (or any two colors plus metallic to go with stickers)
✦ Latex gloves (important)
✦ Cosmetic sponge wedges
✦ Crafter's Pick Brush Strokes gloss finish
✦ 1/2" flat paint brush

How To
1. Wear latex gloves and protect work surface well. DecorIt inks are permanent and dry quickly.
2. Using cosmetic sponge, coat box bottom and lid, inside and out, with Navy. With an almost dry sponge, dab Spring Green, Cranberry, and Gold over surfaces for mottled antique effect.
3. Arrange stickers on box as shown or as desired. Cut or overlap as needed.
4. Dab thin layer of Navy and Gold over stickers, quickly wiping off excess to antique stickers.
5. Following manufacturer's instructions, use flat paint brush to apply two coats Brush Strokes gloss finish. Dry between coats.

What Else
✦ Make boxes in several sizes and present them, nested one inside the other, with a note or piece of jewelry inside the smallest.
✦ Choose a different shape box.
✦ Cut pictures from magazines or catalogs instead of using stickers.
✦ Before applying gloss finish, use a white or gold permanent marker to write a message, names or initials, and a date on the bottom or inside the lid.

Baby's First Christmas

These gentle little ornaments for the new baby's first Christmas could sparkle in a window after the holidays if you would rather keep them out all year long instead of tucking them away.

Assemble

✦ 6-strand embroidery floss listed in color key
✦ Kreinik #16 medium braid and 1/16" metallic ribbon listed in color key
✦ Tapestry needle
✦ 14-count plastic canvas
✦ Pastel pearls from Sulyn
✦ White felt or synthetic suede
✦ Bead needle and white thread
✦ Craft glue

How To

1. Review basic needlepoint instructions on page 12.
2. Stitch ornament. Cut out, leaving one row of plastic on all sides.
3. Hold metallic ribbon at an angle and overcast ends. Stitch three times in outer corners to cover plastic.
4. Using bead needle and white thread, sew pearls to ornament as indicated on diagram.
5. Fold 9" piece of ribbon in half for hanging loop. Sew to back at top center. Trace around ornament on felt or synthetic suede. Cut just inside line so backing won't show from the front.
6. Glue backing to ornament. Use small amount so none seeps through stitching.

What Else

✦ Change the colors and make a "grown up" ornament by using a dramatic combination like gold and black, a traditional combination like red and green, or a jewel tone combination like purple and royal blue. Use gold beads and pearls.
✦ Make a row of ornaments and attach them with swags of beads to decorate the mantel or tree.

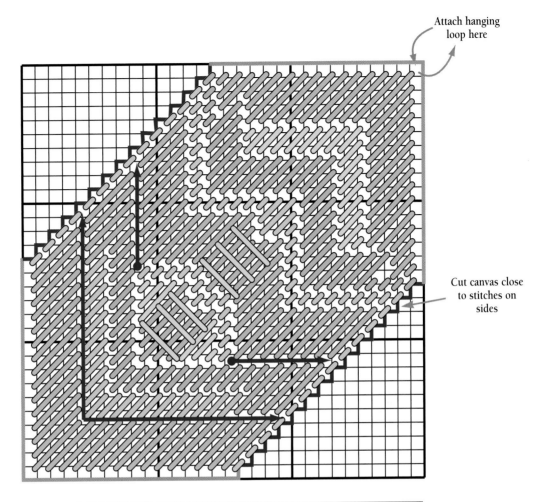

Attach hanging loop here

Cut canvas close to stitches on sides

	Colorway I (Pink)	Colorway II (Blue)
Anchor 6-strand floss	🖊 60 Pink	186 Aqua
Kreinik #16 med braid	🖊 024 Fuchsia	029 Turquoise
	🖊 032 Pearl	032 Pearl
	🖊 029 Turquoise	092 Star Pink
Overcast (ends only)	— 092 Star Pink #16 braid	186 Aqua floss

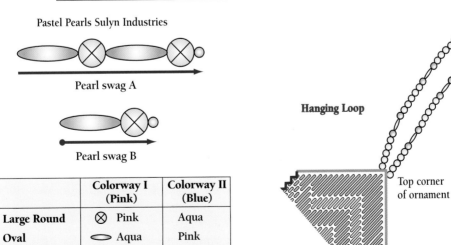

Pastel Pearls Sulyn Industries

Pearl swag A

Pearl swag B

Hanging Loop

Top corner of ornament

	Colorway I (Pink)	Colorway II (Blue)
Large Round	⊗ Pink	Aqua
Oval	⬭ Aqua	Pink
Small Round	○ Aqua	Aqua

A Great Miracle Happened Here

Chanukah, the Jewish holiday celebrating religious freedom, is also known as the Festival of Lights. A tiny amount of oil with which the temple's eternal light was rekindled lasted for a whole week, burning brightly beyond what was possible. To symbolize the miracle, a new candle is added to the menorah, a beautiful candlestick, every night for eight nights. Foods like potato latkes (pancakes) and donuts are fried in oil to continue the symbolism. Children play a game called "dreidel" with a four-sided spinning top. Initials on the sides spell out the first letters of the Hebrew words for the phrase "a great miracle happened here."

Assemble
✦ 6-strand embroidery floss and Kreinik metallic braid listed in color key
✦ 10" square 14-count Aida #8456-5200 Natural from Charles Craft
✦ Tapestry needle
✦ Mat, frame, or finishing supplies as desired
✦ Stretcher bars or embroidery hoop (optional)

How To
1. Review cross-stitch directions on page 12.
2. Stitch design, following chart and color key.
3. Mat and frame as shown or finish as desired.

What Else
✦ Sew a pillow, adding fabric strips to make a larger square.
✦ Finish as a soft wall hanging or display on the padded lid of a wooden box.
✦ Substitute fabric with a different thread count, adjust the number of strands of floss and the size of the metallic braid to make a different size project (almost 8" on 10-count fabric, only 3" worked with one thread on 28-count linen).

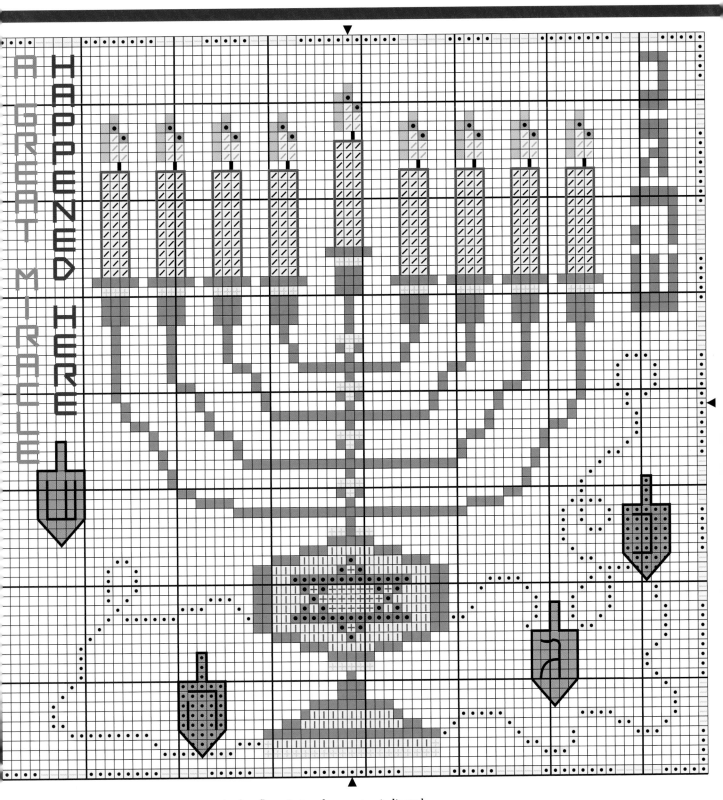

Anchor floss, 3 strands except as indicated

⊡ 188 Turquoise	⊡ 9192 Kreinik #16 braid Light Peach
⊞ 001 Kreinik #16 braid Silver	⊘ 316 Orange
⊟ 877 Dusty Green	⊞ 403 Black
⊘ 158 Pale Blue	⊞ 401 Charcoal
▨ 019 Kreinik #16 braid Pewter	⊡ 186 Lt. Turquoise
▨ 314 Lt. Orange	▨ 218 Dk. Green

▮ 188 backstitch candles 2-strands Turquoise

▮ 188 backstitch "A Great Miracle" Turquoise

▮ 218 backstitch "Happened Here" Dk. Green

▨ 87 Lt. Raspberry

⊡ 89 Dk. Raspberry

▮ 403 backstitch dreidels and candle wicks 2-strands, backstitch letters in dreidels 3-strands

Guardian Angels

For Easter, Christmas, a baptism or christening, these rich sculptural cards will be a gift of meaning and reverence. They are easy enough for children to make as a Sunday school project. One week make the sculpted cross, let them dry, and paint them the following Sunday.

I chose an angel pin that can be removed to wear, but you could glue or sew on an angel button or charm instead.

Assemble

✦ Handmade paper folded into note card (shown, purchased cards #HN02 from Personal Stamp Exchange)
✦ Angel button, pin, or charm (shown, JHB International antique gold Angel Gabriel pin #76001)
✦ Aleene's 3D Accents design paste
✦ Aleene's Create Your Own design template
✦ Aleene's 2" and 4" Trowels and Design Tool
✦ Aleene's Premium Coat acrylics - Deep Wisteria, Deep Classic Gold
✦ Craft knife
✦ Small paint brush
✦ Stencil brush
✦ Tracing paper
✦ Repositionable stencil adhesive

How To

Note: It is normal for handmade paper to ripple slightly.

1. Trace cross and cut out pattern. Trace around pattern on design template and cut out with craft knife. Children will need help with this part of the project. You need one template per person if working in a group.

2. Apply stencil adhesive to back of template. This step is **very** important!

3. Center stencil on front of card. Use 2" trowel to scoop design paste into cross. Smooth with 4" trowel.

4. With design tool, make swirling marks or rows of indentations (refer to photo). If you don't like the effect, smooth with trowel and start again.

5. Lift stencil template straight up to remove. Wash template and allow card to thoroughly dry (overnight is best).

6. Using paint brush and Gold paint, paint the cross. Using stencil brush, dab Gold paint around cross and onto card, using very little paint so texture and color of paper show through. Let paint dry. Wash brushes between colors.

7. Using paint brush and Wisteria, paint raised sides of cross and area right around it. Using stencil brush and very little paint, dab Wisteria around cross and add to gold texture. Wash brushes.

8. Add angel pin, button, or charm to cross.

Reminder: Mail card in padded envelope or small box.

What Else

✦ Frame in a shadow box.
✦ Add a sculpted cross to the top of a box or a bible cover instead of a card.
✦ Reduce the size of the pattern. Use heavy card stock and cut out the cross before painting it. Wear it as a brooch, hang as an ornament, or attach it to a ribbon for a bookmark.

Pockets Full Of Gratitude

Before the turkey and stuffing and pie, take a minute to write messages of gratitude and tuck them in the pockets of this simple wall hanging. Take them out to read them later in the day, or save them for the following year.

Assemble

✦ Fabric and pockets from old jeans
✦ Print or plaid fabric for trim
✦ Bell pull hardware or dowels and finials
✦ Hanging cord, chain, or raffia
✦ Buttons, charms, or other embellishments
✦ Vintage postcards, fronts of Thanksgiving cards, or drawings
✦ Decorative papers
✦ 45mm rotary cutter with deckle blade from Fiskars
✦ Fabric glue
✦ Sewing thread to match fabric trim

How To

1. Cut 10" x 26" rectangle from leg of old jeans. For large family, connect several denim pieces to make bigger rectangle than shown.
2. Hem long sides of rectangle or bind in contrasting fabric. Hem top and bottom to form casing for bell pull hardware or dowels.
3. Arrange pockets on rectangle and glue them on, allowing one or more to extend over edge at bottom.
4. Make a decoration for each pocket from postcards (or color copies of valuable vintage postcards) mounted on layers of decorative paper cut with rotary cutter deckle blade. Glue to pockets.
5. Decorate cards or pieces of paper that fit in pockets with names of family members. Provide markers and pens, stickers, or other supplies so people can write their messages of gratitude.
6. Add hanging cord, chain, or raffia to top of hanging.

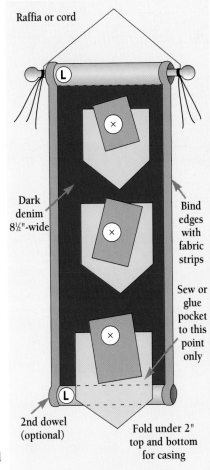

Raffia or cord

Dark denim 8½"-wide

Bind edges with fabric strips

Sew or glue pocket to this point only

2nd dowel (optional)

Fold under 2" top and bottom for casing

Ⓛ 4" strips of light or reverse side of denim

ⓧ Postcard or other decoration

24" length as shown or as desired

What Else

✦ Each year, add messages to a memory album.
✦ Center pockets on denim squares. Add a light color fabric border on four sides of each one, log cabin style. Connect the squares to make a wall hanging. Let family members write messages of gratitude on the border strips with permanent fabric markers. Hide photographs and small gifts in the pockets for children to discover.

Trio Of Trees

Foundation piecing is one of my favorite techniques because it's so easy and fast. There are no templates to cut, so it's perfect for beginners.

This trio of trees uses different sizes of the same block. The ornament is only 3" across. The wall hanging measures two feet, but you could make yours even bigger. The tote bag pocket is 8", roomy enough for a shopping list and keys.

Assemble

✦ Fabric scraps (amount determined by size of block)
✦ Neutral gray sewing thread
✦ Backing fabric size of foundation block pattern
✦ Fun-dation translucent quilt block piecing material size of foundation block (HTC/Handler Textiles)
✦ Pencil or fine line permanent fabric marker
✦ Batting (optional)
✦ Embellishments

Mini Ornament:
✦ Glass Treasures #12190 from Mill Hill
✦ 8" chain
✦ Metallic ribbon bow
Wall Hanging:
✦ Assorted chains (length determined by size of block), tassels, charms, buttons
✦ Heavy duty fusible stabilizer size of foundation block (HTC Crafter's Choice)
✦ Batting (optional)
✦ Cord, rod, or chain for hanging loops as desired
Tote:
✦ Purchased denim bag (shown, denim sling from Bagworks)
✦ Cardinal button from JHB International
✦ Fabric glue (optional)

How To

1. Review foundation piecing directions on page 13.
2. Enlarge pattern to size desired. Trace all lines and numbers on Fun-dation material. Mark background sections with * (two sections next to trunk, two sections next to tree).
3. Piece the block.
4. Sew or glue embellishments to wall hanging after backing it. Chains add weight and the backing helps hold them. Add embellishments to pillows, ornaments, pockets, or other smaller projects before backing them.
5. Finish as wall hanging, lined pocket, or ornament, following directions on page 10. Add batting for extra dimension if desired.
6. Finish by sewing tassels and hanging loops to wall hanging, gluing pocket to tote bag, or sewing hanging loop to ornament.

What Else

✦ Decorate a large wall hanging with a collection of miniature ornaments.
✦ Piece a series of blocks for a quilt.
✦ Make a pot holder or apron pocket.
✦ Add blocks to each end of a long strip of fabric for a table runner.
✦ Back with fabric to match the border and make a pillow.
✦ Make a garland by connecting a row of mini-blocks to each other with wire-edge ribbon bows and swags of cranberry-colored beads.

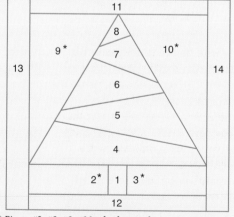

* Pieces #2, #3, #9, #10 = background

Enlarge to 7½" for purse pocket
Enlarge to 15½" for wall hanging
Enlarge to 3" for ornament
Finished project will be the reverse (mirror image) of pattern

Pumpkin Party

Some time in mid-September, I used to start thinking about what I wanted to be for Halloween. Would my mother make me a rabbit costume? She would, and I have the photos to prove it. Would it be cold? A coat over a costume was such a tragedy. Would our beloved Dr. Bernstein up the street give out full-size candy bars as always? Of course! And he let you have a second one if you held your bag out a long time.

Celebrate your Halloween memories with a cross-stitch project that's a treat to make.

Assemble
✦ 6-strand floss listed in color key
✦ Kreinik metallic braid listed in color key
✦ 18-count Zwiegart Aida, color 721 Barn Gray
✦ Black frame with painted candies from Mill Hill
✦ Tapestry needle
✦ Stretcher bars or embroidery hoop

How To
1. Review cross-stitch instructions on page 12.
2. Following chart and color key, stitch the design.
3. Frame as shown or finish as desired.

What Else
✦ Use waste canvas and embroider the design on a canvas treat sack or sweatshirt.
✦ Add fabric strips and make a wall hanging or pillow.
✦ Stitch the design on fabric with a different thread count to enlarge or reduce the size of the project. Adjust number of strands of floss and weight of braid accordingly.

Pattern on page 76

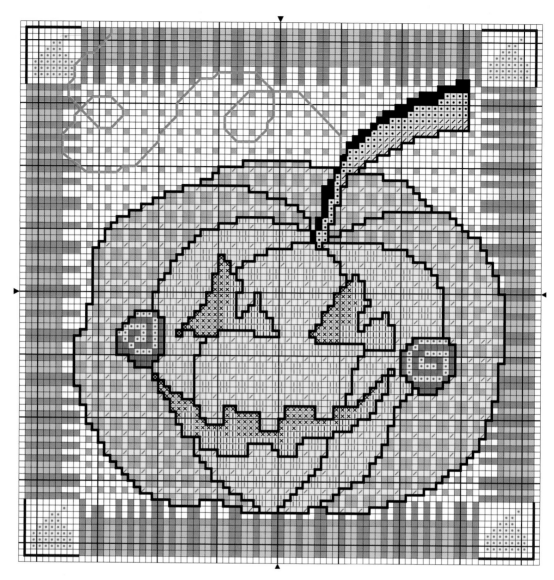

Stitched in Anchor floss (DMC equivalents given) - 3 strands
Note: Opening in frame = 5¹/₂". Center fabric = 6" square over insert board.

Anchor/DMC Colors

- 228/700 Emerald
- 228/700 Emerald backstitch at corners
- 393/3790 Tan
- 906/829 Brass Dark
- 944/869 Wheat Dark
- 360/898 Coffee Dark
- 403/310 Black
- 005 Black Kreinik #8 fine braid
- 1/Blanc Neige White
- 13/817 Salmon Dark

- 027 Orange Kreinik #8 fine braid
- 10/351 Salmon Med.
- 328/3341 Melon
- 382/3371 Fudge
- 3321/946 Blaze
- 238/703 Spring Green Med.
- Vine lines backstitch
  850 Mallard Kreinik #8 fine braid
- 228/700 Emerald backstitch corners 2 strands
- All other outlines (except corners) backstitch
  403/310 Black 2 strands

Chapter Seven

Home & Garden

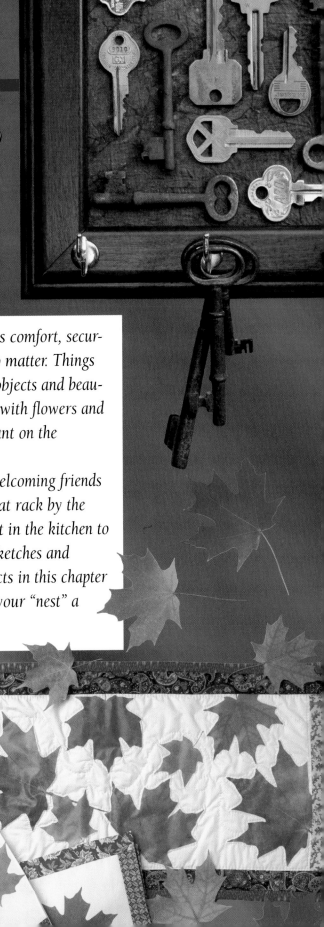

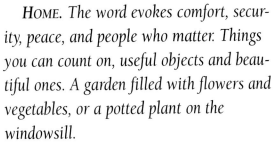

HOME. The word evokes comfort, security, peace, and people who matter. Things you can count on, useful objects and beautiful ones. A garden filled with flowers and vegetables, or a potted plant on the windowsill.

From the guest book welcoming friends at the front door to the coat rack by the pantry, from the place mat in the kitchen to the notebook filled with sketches and pressed flowers, the projects in this chapter are all designed to make your "nest" a special and cozy place.

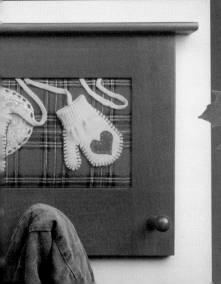

Wooly Gardens

I call my fabric scraps "visual remnants." The wool pieces used as backgrounds for the box and pendant are from coats my grandfather made me many years ago. As I stitched on the firm wool, I could picture him at the cutting table, his confident hands pinning, cutting, and basting. He had beautiful silk labels that said "Sam Fisher, Merchant Tailor." One of them appears in the Collector's Cabinet collage on page 22.

If you have a favorite coat, worn in places but too well-loved to throw away, or some wonderful wool fabric left over from sewing projects, the box and pendant are good ways to extend the memories.

The gardens are embroidered in over-dyed French wool created by a talented colorist named Elaine Warner, owner of Needle Necessities, using just three stitches - feather, satin, and French knots. The pendant takes under an hour to make.

Assemble

✦ 8" square box with 6¾" square opening in lid from Sudberry House
✦ 12" square wool fabric
✦ Four 12" stretcher bars
✦ Two 8" pieces of batting
✦ Over-dyed French Wool from Needle Necessities as listed in color key
✦ Crewel needle

Pendant:
✦ 1⅞" Framecraft oval frame from Mill Hill
✦ #12125 glass butterflies from Mill Hill
✦ Tailor's chalk
✦ Gem-Tac glue

How To

1. Copy pattern guidelines on fabric with tailor's chalk.

2. Staple or tack fabric to stretcher bars.

3. Refer to stitch instructions on page 18. Refer to color key and complete embroidery for box.

4. For pendant, select small area of pattern that fits in oval frame. Use

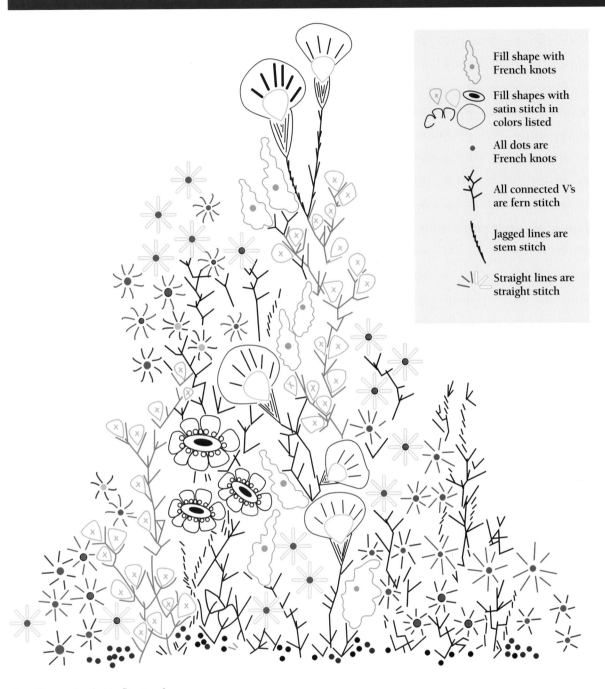

	Fill shape with French knots		
	Fill shapes with satin stitch in colors listed		
•	All dots are French knots		
	All connected V's are fern stitch		
	Jagged lines are stem stitch		
	Straight lines are straight stitch		

Gem-Tac to glue butterflies in place.

5. For box, layer batting pieces on cardboard, under embroidery. Cut away excess.

6. Finish box and pendant following manufacturer's directions.

Option: Have a framer add gold filet at inner edge of box as shown before mounting embroidery.

What Else

✦ Frame and hang on the wall.

✦ Embroider on a garment.

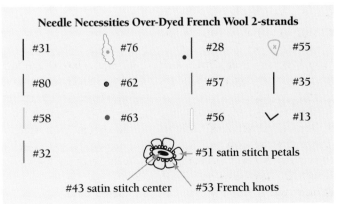

Needle Necessities Over-Dyed French Wool 2-strands

	#31		#76		#28		#55
	#80	•	#62		#57		#35
	#58	•	#63		#56	∨	#13
	#32						

#43 satin stitch center → ← #51 satin stitch petals

#53 French knots

Keys To The Castle

If you have a box full of old keys in a drawer somewhere, pull them out and make a key rack to display them. Rusty old keys look good against a muted batik fabric. I spray painted keys with a suede-textured paint for the safari version.

Assemble
✦ Key rack from Sudberry House (or frame and row of hooks)
✦ Keys
✦ Fabric
✦ Glue - craft, jewelry, and fabric
✦ Buttons with shanks removed, charms, or other embellishments (optional)
✦ Make It Suede tan spray paint from Krylon (for painted keys)

How To
1. Use fabric glue to adhere fabric to cardboard insert that comes with key rack.
2. In a well-ventilated area, spray paint keys in color shown or as desired.
3. Arrange keys on fabric-covered board. Lay frame in place to make sure keys don't extend past frame border. Glue in place with craft glue.
4. For safari rack, use jewelry glue to glue buttons and metal embellishments in place.

What Else
✦ Write memories around the keys in permanent marker.
✦ Use a large chenille needle and yarn or narrow ribbon to sew through a fabric-covered board and tie keys in place with bows.

Good Fortune

I love those little paper fortunes in the cookies that come with a Chinese dinner. Save yours and collect them from your friends - you'll have enough to cover a place mat in no time. Photo transfers allow you to make fabric versions too. Color copies allow you to make a whole set from one collage.

Assemble

✦ Fortune cookie fortunes
✦ 11" x 17" white paper
✦ Craft glue
✦ Photo Effects fabric transfer paper from Hues, Inc.
✦ White fabric
✦ Raspberry rayon machine embroidery thread
✦ Heavy bead wire
✦ Xyron machine (two-sided laminate cartridge, adhesive cartridge) or laminating sheets
✦ Magnets

How To
Place Mats

1. Make matching set by having color copies made of collage.
2. Arrange and glue fortunes to 11" x 17" paper. Cover both sides with laminating sheets or take to professional laminating service.
Note: If you have access to a Xyron machine, use adhesive cartridge to make fortunes into stickers and arrange on 11" x 17" paper. Change cartridge in machine to 2-sided laminate and laminate each mat.

Napkin Rings

1. Take photo transfer paper and fortune-covered paper collage to copy center and have iron-on transfer made.
2. Cut transfer into 2" x 8" strips. Iron on white fabric, leaving 1" between strips.
3. Turn under raw edges and sew to felt, forming ring, or glue to piece of cardboard tube.

4. Cut single fortune from transfer. Iron on white fabric. Back with felt, machine embroider around long sides and short side at end of fortune.
5. Insert small piece of wire in open end so 3D "fortune" will bend. Sew opening.
6. Sew fortune to napkin ring so it sticks out like fortune coming out of cookie.

Magnets

1. Cut color copy or piece of collage 2" x 3½".
2. Laminate and glue onto magnet strip.

What Else

✦ Transfer a collage onto material and sew fabric mats. Use transfers on matching napkins.
✦ Create a collage from fortunes you invent on the computer. Use different typefaces. Include people's names, inside jokes, and personal references.

Garden Memories

Create the look of an Impressionist painting using cosmetic sponge wedges to dab quick-drying inks on a canvas notebook. Use it for garden photographs, sketches, notes and memories, a collection of flower/garden-related postcards, or pressed botanicals.

I practiced and experimented on the inside covers. The inks look bright and shiny on the slick paper, muted and sophisticated on the canvas exterior. Practice on a card or box first if you prefer. Because the inks are opaque and will cover almost anything, including the metal rings, you can recycle and revive an old canvas binder. You can easily cover mistakes too.

Assemble

◆ Ranger DecorIt inks listed in chart or colors you prefer
◆ Wedge-shaped cosmetic sponges
◆ Latex gloves
◆ Canvas or denim covered notebook
◆ White pencil

How To

1. Wear latex gloves and cover work surface. DecorIt inks are permanent and dry quickly.

2. Dab background colors (as shown, purple then gold dappled at random) to completely cover inside and outside of notebook.

3. Practice on inside to get feel of using sponge to create illusion of flowers and leaves. Imagine you are working like an Impressionist painter, dabbing colors rather than painting realistic forms. Dab two colors at once, dipping each side of sponge separately to blend colors.

Note: Each side of sponge wedge will produce a different kind of "dab" (narrow lines, wide marks). Almost dry sponges make light speckled marks; sponges loaded with inks make bright strong marks.

4. Use white pencil to draw guidelines on cover as needed. Follow pattern and color key (refer to photo for ideas), or be playful and invent your own design. It is unlikely you can make an exact duplicate, so don't worry if your flowers look different.

5. The inks are opaque, so you can

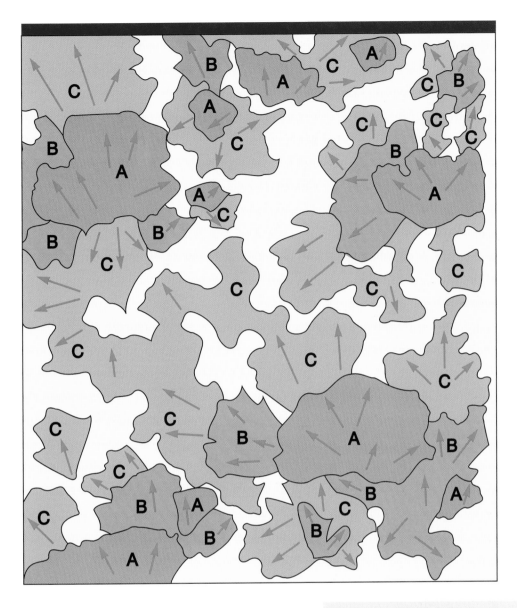

cover mistakes and start again as needed. Let a hint of background colors show through. Many of my "experiments" on inside covers were not repeated on outside.

✦ Fill the notebook with museum memories like postcards and exhibit brochures.

What Else

✦ Decorate section divider pages.

✦ Add your name, dates, a poem, or other lettering.

✦ Make a notebook for each season. Dab snowy winter colors and patterns (silver, periwinkle, white, gray), fall harvest tones (browns, rust, gold, yellow, a hint of chartreuse), summer brights (eggplant, green, tomato red, and more) or lush spring florals (as shown).

Honored Guests

My husband and I can trace the places we've lived and the people who have come to see us by the guest books we've kept near the front door. They're great fun to look at; remembering the brunch for forty to celebrate a birthday or the time when friends came from abroad. I highly recommend the practice.

Assemble
✦ Blank book with lined pages - spiral or hardbound
✦ Fabric or paper to cover front and back
✦ Velvet ribbon, raffia, charms, beads, corrugated paper, or other embellishments
✦ Glue - fabric, craft

How To
Hardbound Book
1. Following diagram, glue fabric and ribbon strip to cover of book. Glue lining to inside covers.
Spiral Bound Book
1. Cut 2"-3" raffia pieces. Fold in half in V-shape and glue to front of book, covering spiral binding.
2. Cover front and back with decorative paper. Glue paper lining inside covers.
3. Add strip of corrugated paper to front, covering V ends of raffia.
4. Glue beaded dangles, narrow ribbon strips, and metal embellishment as shown.

What Else
✦ Center a photograph or drawing of your house on the front of the book.
✦ Cover a pen with matching paper or fabric. Coat it with Liquid Laminate.
✦ Instead of a book, make little cards for people to write on and keep them in a basket.

Diagrams on page 86

My Favorite Flower

I'm a pansy fan, but you can use any flower you want for this little patchwork portrait. I added a touch of embroidery and a few quilting stitches to add dimension, but both are optional.

If you buy the frame first, the size of the patchwork block will be determined by the size of the opening in your frame.

Assemble
✦ Pressed flower
✦ Photo Effects fabric transfer paper from Hues, Inc.
✦ Muslin or off-white fabric
✦ Print fabrics
✦ Embroidery floss to match flower (shown, Anchor floss 314, 102, 119, 291)
✦ Quilt batting and muslin backing (optional)

✦ Wood frame with 5½" opening from Mill Hill
✦ Fabric to cover frame (optional)
✦ Glue - fabric, jewelry
✦ Porcelain buttons to decorate frame (shown, Debbie Mumm from Mill Hill)

How To
1. Press your favorite flower. Take to copy center while colors are fresh and have one or more photo transfers made.
2. Iron transfer on light fabric. Using two strands of floss, embroider straight stitches on flower in selected areas for extra pizzazz. Let transfer show, just add a few stitches.
3. Cut around flower (square or rectangle), leaving border plus 1/2" seam allowance.
4. Sew print fabric strips to top, bottom, and sides for block that fits

opening in frame.
5. Layer over quilt batting and muslin backing. Quilt around flower or add other stitching details, beads, or embellishments.
6. As shown, glue fabric to cover wood frame. Glue porcelain buttons at corners.

What Else
✦ Make a pot holder, curtain border, place mats, or other home décor items.
✦ Incorporate fabric portraits into a Victorian crazy pieced pillow, quilt, or garment.
✦ Use dimensional fabric paint or fine line permanent markers instead of quilting and embroidery.

Patterns on page 86

Spiral bound

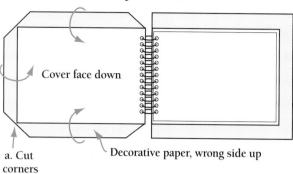

Cover face down

a. Cut corners

Decorative paper, wrong side up

b. Fold and glue excess to inside of cover

Hardbound

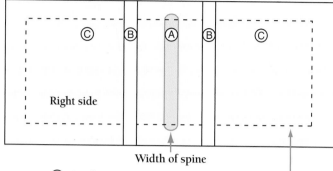

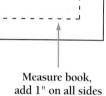

Right side

Width of spine

Measure book, add 1" on all sides

Ⓐ Synthetic suede
Ⓑ Velvet ribbon or other trim
Ⓒ Marble fabric

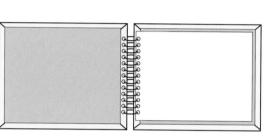

c. Cover with matching or contrasting paper (overlap 1/4")

d. Repeat for back cover

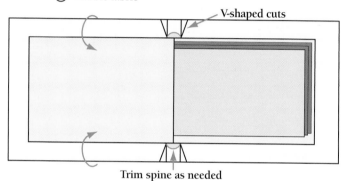

V-shaped cuts

Trim spine as needed

a. Fold and glue long edges
b. Miter, fold, and glue short ends

c. Cover with matching or contrasting paper (overlap 1/4")

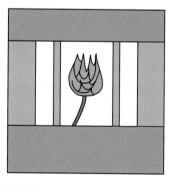

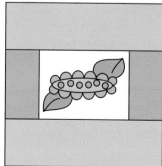

Patterns for "My Favorite Flower" on page 85

A. Start with any shape center piece

B. Add strips at top/bottom, left/right sides to piece into a square

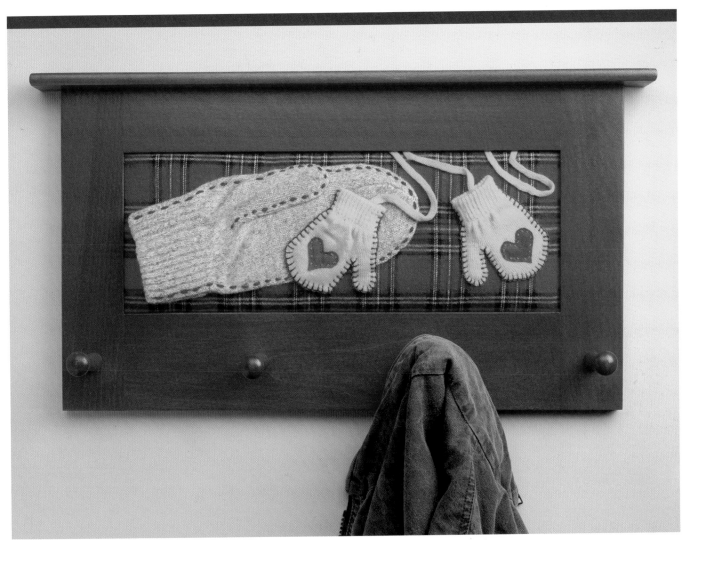

Mitten Memories

What can you do with outgrown mittens or a stray glove that has lost its mate? Let them remind you of romping in the snow or walking to school as they become the focal point for a family coat rack.

Assemble
✦ Shaker coat rack from Sudberry House
✦ Mittens or gloves
✦ 3-ply wool in bright colors from DMC
✦ Background fabric to fit open area in coat rack (shown, plaid flannel)
✦ Chenille needle
✦ Four layers quilt batting to fit cardboard insert provided with coat rack
✦ Fabric glue (optional)
✦ Synthetic suede or wool felt scraps
✦ Buttons, charms, or embellishments as desired.

How To
Sewn Version
1. Mark corners of fabric with pins to show size of opening in coat rack. Arrange mittens and gloves, then pin in place. Refer to photo for ideas.
2. Sew mittens to fabric using chunky embroidery stitches and two strands of wool. Refer to pages 17-18 for blanket stitch and running stitch instructions.
3. Cut small heart shapes from synthetic suede or wool felt to decorate mittens if desired. Sew in place.
4. Layer batting on cardboard insert that comes with coat rack. Follow manufacturer's directions to assemble.
No-Sew Version
1. Use fabric glue instead of embroidery. Glue on hearts, buttons, or other embellishments. Assemble as above.

What Else
✦ Sew the mittens in a row, cuffs at the top. Leave the top open to use as pockets for messages, pencils, keys, and other items.

Fall Foliage

The leaves were particularly beautiful this year. To preserve their exquisite colors, I pressed them and had photo transfers made on the same day. This project would work with ferns, flowers, or any other beautiful botanical.

Assemble

✦ Pressed botanicals
✦ Photo Effects fabric transfer paper from Hues, Inc.
✦ Off-white fabric (amount depends on size of runner and number of napkins)
✦ Print fabrics (amount as above)
✦ Sewing and quilting thread

How To

1. Have photo transfers made while colors on pressed botanicals are bright and fresh.

2. Cut out and arrange photo transfers on off-white fabric. Following manufacturer's directions, transfer them to material.

3. Sew strips of fabric at ends and sides of table runner and around napkins.

4. Turn napkin edges under 1/4" and press. Turn under again and fuse, hand, or machine hem.

5. Baste batting to back of runner panel. Cut fabric for backing and finish like a wall hanging. Refer to page 10 for directions.

6. Hand or machine quilt around leaves, along borders, or as desired.

What Else

✦ Start with a premade tablecloth and napkins.
✦ Add leaves to pillowcases and the border of a flat sheet.
✦ Quilt around a small leaf and insert it in the front of a greeting card.
✦ Create a year-round project by making a different square for each season. Combine them on a quilt or wall hanging or attach the blocks in a row for a table runner.

Chapter Eight
Kids' Stuff

DOLLS AND LITTLE SKETCHBOOKS, a
picture frame made from crumpled lunch
bags, a family message center/bulletin
board, and more. These are things to
make for, and with, the children in your
life. I hope each one brings you a smile
and a hug.

I Can Draw

I made my first doll at age six. I drew her on an old shirt using crayons. My mother ironed the crayons into the material, then sewed the edges and stuffed her. It was magic! I still enjoy making dolls with and for children. Their vision is so open and free. They don't worry if the hands are too big or the head is the right size, they just have fun.

The hula doll started as a paper collage made by my neighbor's granddaughter. I borrowed it, had a photo transfer version made at the copy center, added fusible beads, and sewed it for a surprise.

Assemble

Photo Transfer Version
✦ Photo Effects fabric transfer paper from Hues, Inc.

✦ Collage materials including paper, markers, fabric, string, Beads-2-Fuse, etc.

Direct to Fabric Version
✦ Fabric
✦ Fabric markers
✦ Beads
✦ Dimensional paints
Both
✦ Sewing thread
✦ Fiberfill stuffing

How To

Photo Transfer Version
1. Make a collage on paper or board using gift wrap, fabric scraps, markers, crayons, paint, yarn, raffia, and other flat items.
2. Take collage to copy center and have photo transfer made. Iron transfer on fabric.

3. Add embellishments like Beads-2-Fuse, buttons, or charms over selected areas for dimension before you sew and stuff doll.
Direct to Fabric Version
1. Draw, paint, and appliqué fabric shapes right on piece of fabric. The back of an old shirt is enough for doll and dog as shown.
To Finish Both Versions
1. Cut out doll and backing. Leave at least 1/2" extra fabric on all sides.
2. With pieces wrong sides together so seam allowances are exposed, hand or machine-sew around edges. Use embroidery floss or yarn for chunky running stitch or add machine embroidery. For more finished edges, sew front and back with right sides together, clip curves, and turn right side out. Leave opening at least 3" on one side.
3. Use knitting needle or dowel to push stuffing into arms and legs. Stuff firmly. Sew opening closed.
4. Glue or sew flowers or other large embellishments on finished doll.

What Else

✦ Make animals, cars, boats, and other stuffed toys.
✦ Have a party and let each child create a doll or animal to take home. Ask a friend or two to help with sewing and stuffing. Older children can do that part too.

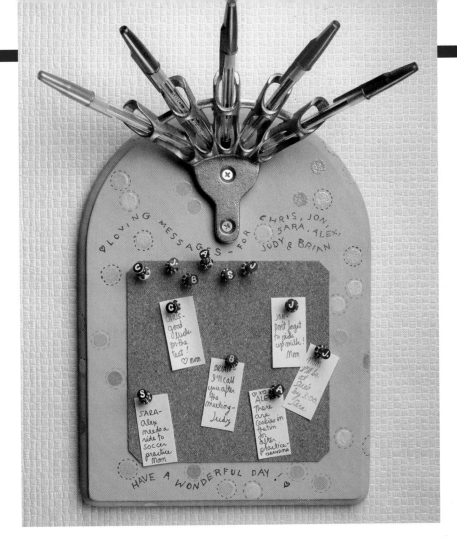

Family Time Message Center

My friend Charles and I were in a hardware store one day when he picked up a metal piece designed to hold five poles and said, "Oh look, this would be great for pens." I loved the idea and designed this project around the flagpole holder.

Photocopy and decorate the "Wish Cards" cards on page 37 to use for your messages.

Assemble

✦ Flagpole holder and screws (I've seen them for up to five poles)
✦ Wood plaque in shape shown or as desired
✦ Make It Suede tan paint from Krylon or color you prefer
✦ Dauber Duo inks in assorted colors from Tsukineko
✦ Iridescent embossing powder
✦ Heat tool

✦ Fine line gel markers in colors to match Daubers, plus black (or acrylic paints and fine point brush)
✦ Cork sheet
✦ Craft glue
✦ Wood pushpins

How To

1. Spread newspapers outdoors or in well-ventilated area. Spray paint wood plaque and let dry. Turn over, spray the back, and let dry. Add second or third coat as necessary.

2. Attach flagpole holder to plaque with wood screws.

3. Cut cork square or rectangle, depending on size and shape of plaque, to fit front of board, leaving 2"-4" border on all sides. Glue cork in place.

4. Randomly stamp Dauber Duo dots over plaque. Complete dots and embossing for one color before adding

the next. While ink is still wet, sprinkle with embossing powder, shake excess on paper to re-use, and emboss with heat tool. Repeat same color ink and add more embossing powder for extra dimension before starting next color.

5. Draw dotted lines around dots using gel markers or paint. Write messages and names as desired. Refer to photo for ideas.

6. Draw initials and decorative doodles on heads and sides of wood pushpins. Use different color for each person. Insert a pen in each flagpole holder.

What Else

✦ Make a plaque for the office or classroom.
✦ Attach a flagpole holder to the wood frame of a premade bulletin board and decorate the frame.

Easy Heirloom Christening Blanket

Okay, moms and aunts and grandmas, get out your crochet hook. This is a very easy christening blanket that will be passed from generation to generation. Add purchased or handmade ribbon flowers to the border squares for an elegant heirloom.

Assemble

✦ J & P Coats Lustersheen 100% virgin acrylic, Art. A.95 sport weight yarn (1¾ oz. balls, amount listed in pattern) or Red Heart Lustersheen 100% virgin acrylic, Art E.600 (8 oz. balls, amount listed in pattern)
✦ Crochet hook size C
✦ Yarn needle
✦ Purchased ribbon rosettes and buds from Wright's (optional)

How To

Cover measures approx. 33" x 40"
Amount: 26¼ ounces
Gauge: Each motif measures 3" x 3". Check your gauge. Use any size hook to obtain the gauge given.

FIRST MOTIF: Ch 6, join with sl st to form a ring. **Rnd 1:** Ch 1, 12 sc in ring, sl st to first sc. **Rnd 2:** Ch 3, *4 dc in first sc, remove lp from hook, insert hook in top of ch 3 and draw dropped lp through - **starting pc st made**, * ch 3, 5 dc in next sc, remove lp from hook, insert hook in first dc and draw dropped lp through - **pc st made**. Rep from * 10 times **more**. Ch 1, dc in top of first pc st - 12 pc sts. **Rnd 3:** Ch 1, sc in lp just formed, * ch 5, sc in next lp. Rep from * end with ch 5, sl st in first sc. **Rnd 4:** Sl st in each of next 3 ch, ch 4, 2 tr in same ch as last sl st, * (4 dc in 3rd ch of next ch 5 lp) twice, ** 5 tr in 3rd ch of next ch 5 lp. Rep form * end at **, 2 tr in same ch as first 2 tr.

Sl st in top of ch 4. **Rnd 5:** Ch 1, 3 sc in same st as sl st, * sc in each of next 12 sts, ** 3 sc in next st. Rep from * end at **. Sl st in first sc. Fasten off.

SECOND MOTIF: Work as for First Motif. Do not fasten off.

Joining rnd: With wrong sides together, *insert hook into back lp of next sc on second motif and into back lp of corresponding sc on first motif, yo and draw through all lps on hook* - **joining sl st made**, joining sl st in each of next 15 sc. Fasten off.

Join 10 more motifs in this manner into a strip - 12 motifs joined. Work first motif of next strip and join to first motif of last strip on one side. Join 2 adjoining sides of next motif to side of last motif and to side of next motif of last strip. Continue in this manner until there are 10 strips of 12 motifs.

Edging: Rnd 1: With right side facing, join yarn with sl st in any corner sc, ch 1, 4 sc in same st, sc evenly around having a multiple of 4 sts across each side and working 4 sc in next 3 corners, sl st to first sc. **Rnd 2:** Ch 1, sc in first sc, * ch 4, 3 tr in same sc, ** skip next 3 sc, sc in next sc. Rep from * end at **. Sl st in first sc. Fasten off. Weave in all ends.
(Courtesy of Coats & Clark)

What Else

✦ Make a second blanket in another color for everyday use.
✦ Increase the size by adding more squares. Create a pillow or small blanket for a doll bed, using fewer squares.

Booties & Bonnet

Beginners take note. These darling little shoes and hat are very easy to crochet. Add purchased or handmade ribbon flowers to match the optional embellishments on the Easy Heirloom Christening Blanket for a beautiful set.

Assemble

✦ J & P Coats Lustersheen 100% virgin acrylic, Art. A.95 sport weight yarn (1¾ oz. balls, amount listed in pattern) *or* Red Heart Lustersheen 100% virgin acrylic, Art E.600 (8 oz. balls, amount listed in pattern)
✦ Crochet hook size C
✦ Yarn needle
✦ Two pearl buttons for shoes
✦ One yard 1"-wide satin ribbon for bonnet

How To

Booties to fit 3 months

Amount: 3/4 ounce
Gauge: In dc - 22 sts and 12 rows = 4". Check your gauge. Use any size hook to obtain the gauge given.

SHOE: Ch 15. **Rnd 1:** 2 dc in 5th ch from hook, dc in each of next 8 ch, 2 dc in next ch, 7 dc in last ch. Working down other side of ch, 2 dc in next ch, dc in each of next 8 ch, 2 dc in next ch, 6 dc in base of ch 4. Sl st to top of ch 3 to join. **Rnd 2:** Ch 3, dc in same sp as sl st, 2 dc in next dc, dc in each of next 10 dc, 2 dc in each of next 9 dc, dc in each of next 10 dc, 2 dc in each of next 7 dc. Sl st to top of ch 3 - 56 sts. **Rnd 3:** Ch 3, dc in each of next 11 dc, ((*yo and draw up a lp in next dc, yo and draw through 2 lps on hook*) *twice, yo and draw through all 3 lps on hook* - **dc dec made**, dc in each of next 2 dc) 6 times, dc in each of next 20 dc. Sl st to top of ch 3. **Rnd 4:** Ch 3, dc in each of next 8 dc, (dc dec over next 2 sts, dc in each of next 2 sts) 6 times, dc in each of next 17 dc. Sl st to top of ch 3. **Rnd 5:** Ch 3, dc in each of next 8 dc, (dc dec over next 2 sts) 8 times, dc in each of next 19 dc. Sl st to top of ch 3. **Rnd 6:** Ch 1, sc in top of ch 3, sc in each dc around. Sl st in first sc. **Rnd 7:** *Ch 3, miss next sc, sl st in next sc. Rep from * to end. Fasten off.

STRAP: Ch 14. Sc in 2nd ch from hook, sc in each of next 11 ch, 4 sc in last ch. Working down other side of ch, ch 2, skip next 2 ch for button lp, sc in each of next 9 ch, 3 sc in next ch. Sl st to first sc. Fasten off.

Sew strap to shoe. Weave in all ends. Sew button in position.

Bonnet to fit 3 months

Amount 1¾ ounces
Gauge: In dc - 22 sts and 12 rows = 4". Check your gauge. Use any size hook to obtain the gauge given.

BACK: Ch 24. **Row 1 (right side):** Dc in 3rd ch from hook, dc in each ch to end. Ch 3, turn - 22 sts. **Row 2:** Skip first dc, dc in each st to end. Ch 3, turn. Rep last row 9 more times. **Row 13:** Skip first dc (*yo and draw up a lp in next dc, yo and draw through 2 lps on hook*) *twice, yo and draw through all 3 lps on hook* - **dc dec made**, dc in each st to last 3 sts. Dc dec over next 2 sts, dc in top of ch 3. Ch 3, turn. **Row 14:** Skip first dc, dc dec over next sts, dc in each st to last 3 sts, dc dec over next 2 sts, dc in top of ch 3 - 18 sts. Fasten off.

TOP AND SIDES: With right side of work facing join yarn with sl st to lower right corner of Back. **Row 1:** Ch 3, work 24 dc evenly up side of Back, dc in each dc across last row of Back, work 24 dc evenly down rem side of Back - 66 sts. Ch 3, turn. **Row 2:** Skip first dc, dc in each dc to end. Ch 3, turn. Rep last row 14 more times omitting turning ch at end of last row. **Next Row:** Ch 1, sc in each dc to end. Ch 1, turn. **Next Row:** * Ch 3, skip next sc, sc in next sc. Rep from * to last st, sc in last st. Fasten off.
Fold last 3 rows of work to right side to form brim. Sew loosely in position at lower edges.

LOWER BAND: With right side of work facing, join yarn with sl st at lower left corner fold. Work 22 sc evenly along Side edge working through both thicknesses of Brim, in rem lps of foundation ch of Back work (sc in each of next 2 ch, skip 1 ch) 7 times, sc in last ch. Work 22 sc evenly along rem Side edge working through both thicknesses of Brim - 59 sc. Ch 1, turn. **Next Row:** Sc in each st to end. Ch 1, turn. Rep last row 4 more times. Fasten off.

Weave in all ends. Sew ribbon ends to sides of Band, adjust ribbon length and trim ends diagonally. (*Courtesy of Coats & Clark*)

What Else

✦ Appliqué hearts to the soles of the shoes.
✦ Choose a different color.

Lunch Bags & Lizards

This project is lots of fun to do on a rainy day. I started with a wood frame, but you could use a cardboard mat. The Liquid Laminate coating makes the frame durable. Make sure you use jewelry glue to hold the plastic critters in place.

Assemble

✦ Brown paper bags
✦ Flat wood frame or cardboard mat
✦ Liquid Laminate from Beacon
✦ Craft glue
✦ Hemp or twine
✦ Plastic lizards or other critters
✦ Gem-Tac glue
✦ Glass to cover photo (optional)
✦ Scissors with small sharp points (younger children will need help with step 3)
✦ Paint brush

How To

1. Cut open a paper bag. Crumple, then smooth out, leaving lots of creases and wrinkles. Make sure paper is 2" bigger than frame.

2. Spread thin layer of craft glue on front of frame. Lay frame face down on crumpled paper. Turn frame over and smooth paper. Make sure there are no big bumps, but leave creases and wrinkles.

3. Turn frame face down on work surface. Cut window in middle of frame, leaving 1" paper around wood. Cut angled slits at corners. Fold paper to back of frame and glue. Wrap paper like a package at top, bottom, and sides of frame. Glue in place.

4. Brush two coats Liquid Laminate over paper-covered frame, letting dry between coats.

5. Glue hemp or twine round and round frame, some lines straight, some lines loopy and droopy. Make sure twine isn't too tight so you can still insert glass and photo.

6. Use Gem-Tac to glue lizards or other critters to frame.

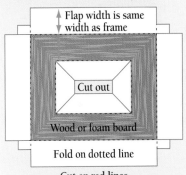

↕ Flap width is same
width as frame

Cut out

Wood or foam board

Fold on dotted line

Cut on red lines

a. Frame, face down on back of crumpled bag
b. Cut flaps with tabs on long sides.
c. Cut flaps without tabs on short sides
d. Fold and glue b, then c
e. Cut center, stop angled cuts just short of corner

What Else

✦ Glue bugs around the frame. Let a spider hang from a long string.
✦ Paint or rubber stamp designs on the paper bag before you put it on the frame.
✦ Crumple a black paper shopping bag instead of a lunch bag. The creases will crack and form spooky white lines.

My Little Books

Give a small spiral bound note-book with a bright cover, an assort-ment of stickers or stamps, scissors that cut different designs, glitter, markers, and other crafty supplies to a young friend and let him/her decorate the front. Make one for yourself too. I covered one with fruit and veggie stickers to use for grocery lists. It gets smiles and compliments each time I take it out of my purse.

Chapter Nine
This & That

THE OBJECTS WE SAVE and the memories they evoke take many forms. A child's party shoes. A collection of rhinestone pins. An old cigar box. Each conjures visions of people, events, and places. Here is a potpourri of projects devoted to "this and that." May it spark your creativity and stir up lots of ideas.

Buttons & Buds

Sometimes my button jar includes a matching set, removed from a garment so well loved that the fabric wore out. To show off a row of my favorites, I decided to decorate a tote bag. For smaller buttons, center each one on a flower.

Assemble

✦ Natural canvas tote (or color of choice)
✦ Buttons
✦ Kreinik #4 extra fine metallic braid #221 Antique Gold
✦ Sewing thread to match tote
✦ Silk flowers
✦ Fabric glue (optional)

How To

1. Arrange buttons and flowers to your liking along top edge of tote bag. Center small buttons, space large buttons between them.
2. Remove stems and plastic pieces from flowers as needed.
3. Sew flowers in place with thread to match tote. Sew buttons in place using metallic braid, doubled in needle.
4. For a no-sew version, remove shanks from buttons and hold everything in place with fabric glue. Do not remove shanks or use glue on valuable buttons that you may want to remove for another use.

What Else

✦ Make a pillow, spacing buttons and buds in a grid pattern like the shell pillow on page 48.
✦ Arrange buttons and flowers in a pattern instead of a straight row.
✦ Stencil or paint a row of flower shapes and sew a button to the center of each.

Painted Treasure Box

Unless you look very closely, you won't recognize that under all of the patterns lies a humble slide-top cigar box. This project requires some patience and time, but the design is so busy that you don't need to worry about accuracy. Washington artist Jo Rango painted this box for me as a gift. I use it to store my souvenir ball-point pen collection.

Assemble
+ Cigar box
+ Acrylic paint - black, red
+ Fine paint brush
+ Varnish (optional)

How To
1. Trace around sides, top, and bottom of box on lightweight (typing) paper to make practice sheets if desired. Doodle patterns like small checkerboard squares, rows of lines, ovals and dots, simple animals, people, houses, trees, etc.
2. Since your box might be a different shape or size, refer to photograph for ideas rather than specifics.
3. Paint inside and outside of box, covering every inch with pattern. If there are words on box, paint straight lines like grass in the garden over them and lettering will disappear.
4. Varnish with matte or gloss finish.

What Else
+ Paint a paper maché box or a round cookie tin.

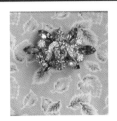

Show & Tell Squares

I like having my pin collection on the wall instead of in a box. I made my hanging big enough to accommodate future acquisitions. Each time I look at the sparkling shapes, I remember who they are from or where I bought them. The title "Show And Tell" is to celebrate childhood days when it was okay to show off a little bit every now and then.

Just like the Father's Day chess and checker game board on page 66, this project is stitched on a preprinted fusible grid. Even beginners and nonquilters will get perfect results.

Assemble
✦ Quilt-Fuse preprinted fusible quilt block backing from HTC/Handler Textiles (amount determined by size of hanging selected, see below)
✦ Backing fabric same size as Quilt-Fuse
✦ 4" fabric squares
✦ Sewing thread
✦ Beads, tassels, ribbons, other embellishments
✦ Crafter's Choice fusible stabilizer from HTC/Handler Textiles
✦ Twisted cord for hanging loops (amount determined by diameter of hanging rod)

How To
1. Quilt-Fuse is printed with a 2" grid. Four squares equals one 4" block. You need one 4" print fabric square for each block. I made a long vertical rectangle. Choose size and

shape you like and purchase right amount of Quilt-Fuse.
2. Lay out squares on sticky (fusible) side of Quilt-Fuse, using printed lines as guide. When you like arrangement, iron to fuse in place. Following manufacturer's directions, turn panel over, fold, and sew all printed parallel lines in one direction. Turn and repeat in second direction.
3. Fuse backing fabric to stabilizer.
4. Fold twisted cord hanging loop pieces in half. Pin them at intervals across right side of panel across top. Raw (cut) ends extend into seam allowance.
5. Finish as a wall hanging. See instructions on page 10.
Option: Instead of loops and rod, sew Velcro dots or small plastic rings to upper corners (on back) to hang.
6. Sew flat beads between squares at intervals as shown to hold backing in place. Add ribbon, tassels, or other embellishments as desired.
7. For softer hanging, omit stabilizer and use quilt batting instead.

What Else
✦ Use country plaid fabrics and display a collection of campaign buttons.
✦ Instead of a soft hanging, pad with three layers of quilt batting, back with board, and frame.
✦ Make bigger squares and display award ribbons or larger items.
✦ Make smaller squares to display souvenir pins or a button collection.

Before & After Party Shoes

Since little feet almost always grow before party shoes get worn out, how about giving special occasion footwear more than one life? First decorate the shoes for a holiday or birthday party or to wear out to dinner. Then turn the shoes into pincushions for your sewing room or to display hatpins on the dresser. Or start with brand new shoes and just make the pincushions - they're excellent for a craft fair or church bazaar.

Assemble

For Both
✦ Plain shoes (shown, black velvet and red patent)
✦ Craft glue
✦ Fabric and batting for cushion

Red Shoes
✦ Coarse red glitter
✦ Masking tape
✦ Red thread
✦ Two 12" pieces 2"-wide red ribbon
✦ Two 12" pieces 2"-wide white ribbon

Black Shoes
✦ Ribbon colors as shown (from Offray) or as desired
✦ Two 7" pieces 1½"-wide mauve wire-edge ribbon
✦ Eighteen 3" pieces 5/8"-wide blue ombre wire-edge ribbon
✦ Six small velvet leaves

How To

Red Shoes
1. Protect strap, sole, and fabric edge of shoes with masking tape. Cover shoes with glue and coarse red glitter, shaking off excess. When shoes dry, carefully add more glue and glitter to any bare areas. Remove tape.
2. For bows, make each 12" piece of ribbon into a loop. With thread, gather it in the middle with the cut ends touching in the center. Turn the sides under on the 3" piece and cover the gathering thread to make bow appear "tied." Sew raw edges at back.
3. Glue bows to strap of shoe.
4. To finish as a pincushion, cut piece of fabric as shown in diagram. Gather with running stitch around roll of batting (see diagram). Put padded roll in shoe as if it were a foot, easing it down into toe area and smoothing gathers.

Black Shoes

1. Make eight folded petals (see page 17) and one drooping bow (see diagram) for each shoe. Rumple along wires so they look old and Victorian. Wrinkle velvet leaves.

2. Starting at sides of shoe and working toward middle, glue petals and leaves to shoe. Glue bow over raw edges at center (see diagram).

3. To finish as pincushion, see step 4 for Red Shoes.

What Else

✦ Buy some dynamite grown-up pumps at a thrift shop and make a high-heel pincushion.

✦ Turn a child's sneaker into a funky pincushion using plaid fabric to cover the padded roll. Decorate the shoe with dimensional paint.

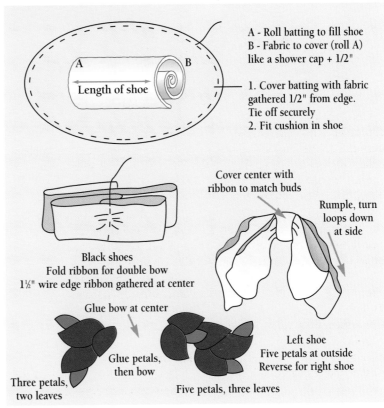

A - Roll batting to fill shoe
B - Fabric to cover (roll A) like a shower cap + 1/2"

1. Cover batting with fabric gathered 1/2" from edge. Tie off securely
2. Fit cushion in shoe

A

B

Length of shoe

Cover center with ribbon to match buds

Rumple, turn loops down at side

Black shoes
Fold ribbon for double bow
1½" wire edge ribbon gathered at center

Glue bow at center

Glue petals, then bow

Three petals, two leaves

Five petals, three leaves

Left shoe
Five petals at outside
Reverse for right shoe

Cameo Appearance

Nestle a piece of jewelry, a coin from a far-off place, a lock of hair, or a lucky charm into a cameo-topped box stitched in no time. If you are feeling really frazzled but you like the project, just make the top piece and glue it on a fabric-covered box.

A color key is given for the copper box. Other combinations are shown to inspire you to choose your own favorite colors and try something different.

Assemble

✦ 6-strand floss, metallic ribbon, and braid listed in color key
✦ Flat-backed cameo or other embellishment
✦ 14-count plastic canvas
✦ Synthetic suede and fabric (lining and optional flat base)
✦ Pebble beads (for feet)
✦ Craft glue
✦ Cardboard

How To

1. Refer to basic needlepoint instructions on page 12.
2. Stitch top and sides of lid and sides of base. Cut unworked plastic piece for bottom of base.
3. Cut synthetic suede pieces for lining, using plastic as pattern.
4. Overcast lid pieces together. Overcast base pieces together.
5. Cut four pieces of cardboard 1/4" taller and 1/16" narrower than sides of

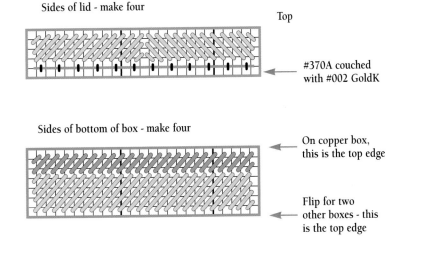

Connect and overcast
pieces with Kreinik 1/16"
metallic ribbon, #021
Copper

A = Anchor floss
K = Kreinik #16 med braid

Lid

Inner row #370A
couched with 2122K

Outer row #370A
couched with #002 GoldK

#883A

#880A

#2122
CurryK

Sides of lid - make four

Top

#370A couched
with #002 GoldK

Sides of bottom of box - make four

On copper box,
this is the top edge

Flip for two
other boxes - this
is the top edge

base. Cover both sides with synthetic
suede or fabric. Glue inside box (these
pieces stick up to hold lid in place).
6. Glue synthetic suede or fabric to
inside of lid and base.
7. Glue cameo to lid. Glue three
pebble beads to each corner as feet, or
cover a piece of plastic two rows larger
than bottom of box with synthetic
suede and glue it in place as a base.

What Else

✦ Make a bigger box by using 5- or 7-
count plastic canvas and heavier yarn,
ribbon, and braids.
✦ To make a larger box on the same
size canvas, repeat the lid four times
like patchwork. Cut longer strips for
the sides of the lid, bottom, and base.
✦ To make earrings or a brooch, stitch
the center square and turn it point up
like a diamond. Position the cameo to
match the new direction of the square.
Add a bead fringe on the bottom two
edges. Back with synthetic suede and
glue on earring backs or a pin finding.

Suggested color combinations (shown on other boxes)		
	Colorway I	Colorway II
Needle Necessities over-dyed 6-strand floss	#123 #141	#186 #149
Anchor	#871 #261 #851 #870 #388	#1020 #1034 #871 #68 #1036

Chapter Ten

Cards, Mats, Frames & Certificates

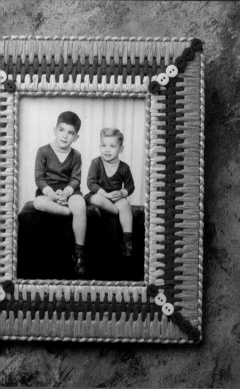

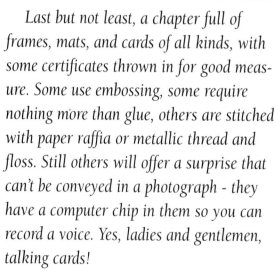

Last but not least, a chapter full of frames, mats, and cards of all kinds, with some certificates thrown in for good measure. Some use embossing, some require nothing more than glue, others are stitched with paper raffia or metallic thread and floss. Still others will offer a surprise that can't be conveyed in a photograph - they have a computer chip in them so you can record a voice. Yes, ladies and gentlemen, talking cards!

When you take this book to the copy center to reproduce the certificates, show them this page giving the author's permission to make copies for your own noncommercial use.

Making A Good Impression

Excuse the pun, but these mats are created by making a good impression - on foam blocks that have been heated and pressed with textured objects like shells or wire. Everything in your house, yard, or office will become a potential source of texture.

Here's the theory: There are two layers - the background and the pattern. The background is created by brushing color onto paper mats using rubber stamp ink pads. They can be pale and muted like the turquoise/pink version with the trio of ladies, or deep and rich like the rust/wine/orange/gold of the others. Then the texture block is stamped and embossed. That's all there is to it.

When I make a block I like, I keep it to use again and again. If you make one you don't like, just heat the block and the impression will disappear so you can reuse it.

Assemble
✦ Colorbox Petalpoint pigment ink pads from Clearsnap
✦ Magic Stamp (PenScore) foam blocks from Clearsnap
✦ Heat tool
✦ Precut mats from Savage Universal
✦ Embossing powders (iridescent or clear)

How To
1. Use ink pads to brush background colors on mat. Combine as suggested or as desired. Let ink dry.
2. Follow manufacturer's directions to heat and emboss block of Magic Stamp foam using wire, lace, shells, basket, chair seat, or any other texture that might make an interesting pattern.
3. Ink embossed block and stamp repeatedly over mat's surface. While ink is wet, sprinkle embossing powder over pattern, shaking off excess to save for another project.
4. Use heat tool to raise embossing powder.
Option: Layer small decorated mat over larger plain one and add tassels. Frame in shadow box or use spacers under glass so embellishments won't get crushed.

What Else
✦ *Everything!* Paper clips, soles of shoes, uncooked pasta, spools, pebbles, leaves, twigs, handprints, jewelry, and more all make excellent textures to stamp.

Raffia Frame

I designed this frame to look like a handwoven basket. It can be made in any size by extending the chart and repeating the pattern till it's as big as you want. Stitched on rigid plastic canvas, it needs no blocking. Just back it to hang or add an easel to stand on a desk or mantel. In masculine colors, it's the perfect way to show off the guys in your life but the Raffia Accents come in pastels and lively floral tones, too.

Assemble

✦ Sixteen burgundy 3/8" diameter buttons
✦ Eight 3/8" cream/ivory buttons
✦ Raffia Accents from Plaid:
    four pkgs. #37862 Orange
    three pkgs. #37864 Burgundy
three pkgs. #37860 Golden Natural
two pkgs. #37861 Brown
✦ 10" x 12" piece 7-count plastic canvas
✦ #16 Tapestry needle
✦ Craft glue

How To

1. Following chart and color key, stitch frame pattern. Keep paper raffia smooth and flat. Work with short lengths to keep it from fraying.
2. Cut out frame, leaving one row of plastic on all edges. For two-color edge, overcast every other hole with Golden Natural raffia. Overcast with Brown raffia to fill remaining holes.
3. Glue photo in place. Back with fabric-covered card stock. Add easel to display on desk or hanging loop to display on wall.
Option: To change photo, make a felt or synthetic suede pocket on back. Leave top edge of pocket open for access.

What Else

✦ Enlarge the frame by repeating the pattern to the desired size.
✦ To use four colors instead of three, divide the Burgundy portion of the pattern into two bands.
✦ Combine Light Lavender, Dark Lavender, Pink, and Light Olive Green for Easter; Red, Dark Green, and Golden Natural for Christmas; or create a combination that goes with your décor.

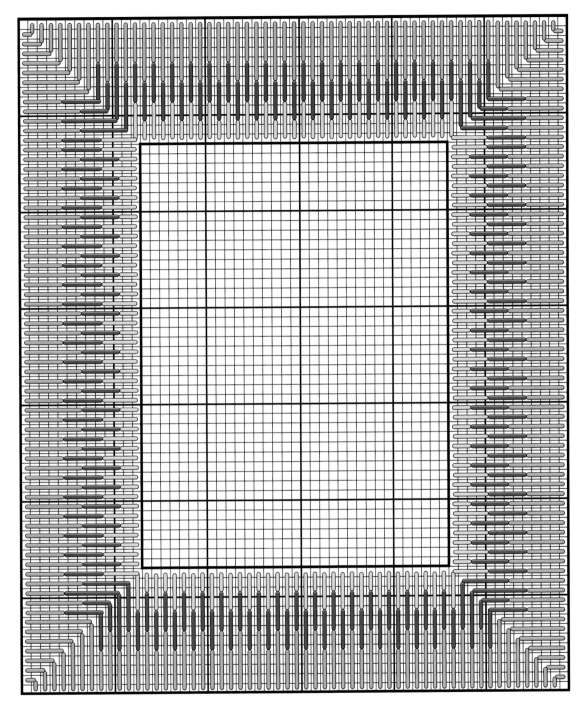

Plaid Raffia Accents
Overcast edges alternating every other stitch #37860 Golden Natural and #37861 Brown

37860 Golden Natural
37864 Burgundy
37862 Orange

Backyard Botanicals

Making handmade paper is a great way to recycle. The green cards were created out of junk mail and snippets of thread. The purple one includes pieces of a bright paper napkin. I used fresh ferns to emboss background stamp blocks, inked and printed them, then used dried ferns in the collage. Repetition enhances the design and adds dimension.

Assemble

✦ Handmade paper (made with the Papermill from Arnold Grummer) or purchased cards
✦ 2½" x 3½" Magic Stamp (PenScore) moldable foam block from Clearsnap
✦ Heat tool
✦ Dried ferns, flowers, leaves, plus one fresh (not dried) fern
✦ Gold and black Colorbox pigment ink pads from Clearsnap
✦ Buttons (with shanks removed), charms, or other flat-backed embellishments
✦ Craft glue
✦ Microfleur microwave flower press (optional)

How To

1. Press and dry ferns, flowers, and leaves. I used the Microfleur press in my microwave oven.
2. Make handmade paper or purchase interesting sheets of card stock. Cut and fold cards into different sizes and shapes.
3. Following manufacturer's instructions, heat foam block and emboss with fresh fern or leaf to create reverse image stamp. Using gold ink with touch of black, stamp several sheets of white paper. Let ink dry.
4. Press same fresh fern or leaf into black ink with touch of gold. Use fern to stamp over printed reverse image,

offset in another position so you see both positive and reverse images.
5. On dark paper, use gold ink to print reverse block. Do not stamp inked leaf.
6. Cut small square or odd-shaped pieces of stamped background and other papers. Arrange on folded cards and glue in place.
7. Arrange dried botanicals and embellishments and glue in place. *Note:* Cards are fragile, so mail in a box.

What Else

✦ Mat and frame the collage. Add spacers under glass so botanicals don't get crushed or frame in a shadow box.
✦ Use purchased rubber stamps for the background patterns. Textures and leaves are readily available.

Postcard Collage

The message side of postcards can sometimes be as interesting as the pictures. The vintage postcards I've collected with beautiful handwriting and gentle messages take me to other times and places. I used color copies, reduced in size, so I didn't have to cut up the originals for my collage. Display in a shadow box to protect dimensional embellishments.

Assemble
✦ Precut mat from Savage Universal
✦ Lace and trims, charms, or other embellishments
✦ Color copies of postcards, message side (reduced to 4" across)
✦ Craft glue or double-faced adhesive sheets

How To
1. Arrange postcards at angles around opening in mat, allowing them to extend past edges of mat. Cut sections to fit. Secure with glue or double-faced adhesive sheet.

2. To give vintage look to new trims, soak in strong tea for half hour. Rinse and dry.

3. Arrange trims and lace and glue in place.

What Else
✦ Combine the picture and message sides of postcards in a collage.
✦ Embellish with small photographs, stickers, or canceled stamps in addition to or instead of lace.

Pansy Poses

I can't get enough pansies. These frames are made with stickers from the same company as the pre-cut corrugated frame used for the three-hole version. I cut an opening in the backing board to make a second frame and used the rectangle from the opening to make the card. Not a scrap wasted!

The finishes are different. One frame is high gloss, the other matte. Choose your favorite or make both.

Assemble
✦ Pansy stickers and precut frame from Sticker Planet
✦ Colorbox PetalPoint ink pads from Clearsnap - Gold, Turquoise, Purple, Olive Green
✦ 45mm rotary cutter with deckle blade from Fiskars
Card
✦ Velvet leaves
✦ Card stock
✦ Craft glue
✦ Chenille needle
✦ Kreinik 080HL #16 medium braid
Frames
✦ Matte acrylic spray or EnviroTex Lite pour-on laminate

How To
Frames
1. Cut rectangular opening in backing board that comes with precut frame. Set aside rectangular cutout to use for card.
2. Use ink pad to brush frames with Turquoise to cover. Three-hole frame is brushed with Gold and Olive, one-hole frame is brushed with Gold and Purple (Purple at edges only). Use fingers to spread and dapple colors.
3. Arrange stickers on frames. Brush lightly with Gold and Turquoise ink, wiping off excess for an antique effect.
4. To seal frames, spray with matte acrylic or coat with EnviroTex Lite pour-on laminate.
5. Display on easel or hang.
Card
1. Use deckle blade on rotary cutter for edges and corners of cardboard rectangle. Color, decorate with stickers, and antique like frame.
2. Attach collage to foam board for dimension. Position on handmade paper rectangle.
3. Decorate with long stitches using metallic braid.
4. Wrinkle velvet leaves for vintage effect. Glue around pansy collage.

What Else
✦ Cut your own simple shape with windows for photographs.
✦ Instead of stickers, use cutouts from magazines and catalogs. Seal the surface with thinned down white glue before applying finish.

Vintage Velvet

Make the perfect mat or frame for an old-time photograph or a new one you've had processed as a sepia tone print.

Assemble
✦ Precut mat or flat unfinished wood frame
✦ Velvet leaves (available from Ruban et Fleur)
✦ Craft glue
✦ Paint to complement velvet leaves (for wood frame)

How To
1. For wood frame, paint to match darkest color in velvet leaves. Sides of frame are not covered with leaves and will show.
2. Remove leaves from stems. Overlap as shown and adjust spacing as needed. Glue in place.
3. To use as mat, frame in shadow box or use spacers under glass so leaves don't get crushed.

What Else
✦ Intersperse leaves with occasional silk flowers.
✦ Use white satin leaves from the bridal department for a wedding or anniversary memento.
✦ Laminate a photograph. Mount it on heavy board. Glue the leaf border directly to the photo. Attach an easel back.

Certificates Of Appreciation & Recognition

The easiest project in the book, all you have to do is have copies made, fill in the certificates, and put them in an envelope or frame. You can color and embellish the black and white ones or add surface embellishments to either version. Tell the copy center you have the author's permission to make as many copies as you want for personal, noncommercial use.

Assemble

✦ Black and white or color copies of certificates
✦ Optional embellishments, stickers, flowers, buttons, etc.

✦ Craft glue
✦ Markers and colored pencils
✦ 8" x 10" frame
✦ Permanent black marker or press-on lettering

How To

1. Make photocopies of certificates.
2. Color black and white copies with markers or pencils.
3. Glue on photographs, buttons, stickers, flowers, lace, charms, or other embellishments.
4. Fill in message with permanent marker or press-on lettering.

What Else

✦ Enlarge or reduce the size of the certificate to create a wall- or wallet-sized one.

Certificate of Recognition

To:

For:

From:

Date:

Certificate of Recognition

To:

For:

From:

Date:

If Cards Could Talk

The best part of this project is the part that can't be seen in a photograph. There is a computer chip in the card that lets you record a message that plays each time the card is opened. It can be re-recorded to change the words or made permanent so the voice can't be accidentally erased. The card has an opening in the front to display a photograph, postcard, or drawing.

Assemble

✦ Voice Express greeting cards
✦ Small, natural color premade fabric yo-yos from Wimpole Street Creations (or make your own)
✦ Craft glue
✦ Ribbons, buttons without shanks, or trims as desired

How To

1. Slip photo into front of greeting card.
2. Arrange and glue yo-yos and trims as shown or as desired as border on front and sides of card.
3. Add buttons, charms, flowers, or other dimensional embellishments.
4. Decorate inside of card with markers, stickers, and other flat embellishments.
5. Following manufacturer's directions, record your message.

What Else

✦ Get a group of friends together and have everyone sing Happy Birthday into the card.
✦ Use rubber stamps, embossing, stickers, markers, or other decorations.
✦ Voice Express also makes Voice Over and Voice-Plus to attach to picture frames and scrapbook pages. You'll love them all, and they don't pay me to say so!

Someone Special

When quick-to-stitch needlepoint borders are glued on readily available freestanding acrylic frames, they are ready to display on a mantel, desk, or dresser. There is a chart for both color combinations, but you can substitute your own choices.

Assemble

✦ 6-strand embroidery floss, Kreinik #16 medium braid and 1/16" metallic ribbon in color key
✦ 14-count plastic canvas
✦ Tapestry needle
✦ 3½" x 5½" vertical format freestanding acrylic frame
✦ Craft glue

How To

1. Review needlepoint instructions on page 12.
2. Following chart and color key, stitch frame. Cut out, leaving one row of plastic on all sides.
3. Overcast edges with metallic ribbon held at an angle. Stitch three times in outer corners to cover plastic.
4. Insert photo in frame. Glue needlepoint border to front of frame, making sure to position so bottom edge rests on table.

What Else

✦ Use as a mat within a frame.
✦ Back with a magnet to display on a metal surface.
✦ Glue to a greeting card.
✦ On a light color tote bag or garment, stitch the pattern using cross-stitch on waste canvas instead of needlepoint. Backstitch around edges. Iron a photo transfer in the center area.

(Except as noted) Anchor 6-strand

Colorway I (dog) Needle Necessities over-dyed floss		Colorway II (man in tuxedo) Needle Necessities over-dyed floss
#135 Bali Hai		#153 Razzle Dazzle Red
#851 Dark Teal		#403 Black
#280 Pale Olive		#815 Dark Gray
#848 Pale Teal		#869 Pale Mauve
#102 Purple		#872 Dark Mauve
#110 Lavender		#398 Pale Gray
#023 Lilac		Kreinik #16 med braid #025 Gray
#085 Peacock		Kreinik #16 med braid #003 Red
#045 Confetti Gold		Kreinik #16 med braid #061 Ruby

Overcast outer edges Kreinik 1/16" metallic ribbon

#018 Navy	#005 Black

Overcast top and left side of center opening Kreinik 1/16" metallic ribbon

#012 Purple	#025 Gray

Overcast bottom and right side of center opening

#025 Confetti Gold	#061 Ruby

Paperweight Frames

Stitch a paperweight with an opening for a photograph or to frame any small cherished collectible. For the desk or dresser or to sit by the computer, these will make memorable gifts.

Assemble

✦ 6-strand embroidery floss, Kreinik metallic braids, ribbon listed in color key
✦ Rectangular glass paperweight from Yarn Tree
✦ Tapestry needle
✦ 14-count plastic canvas

How To

1. Review needlepoint instructions on page 12.
2. Following chart and color key, stitch frame. Carefully cut opening, leaving one row of plastic on all edges.
3. Overcast around photo opening and sides of frame with metallic ribbon held at an angle. Stitch three times at outer corners to cover plastic.
4. Discard cardboard insert that comes with paperweight. Adhere needlepoint to adhesive-backed cork and place cork on bottom of glass, following manufacturer's directions.

What Else

✦ Finish as a magnet instead of under glass.
✦ Glue to the front of a greeting card or lid of a treasure box.

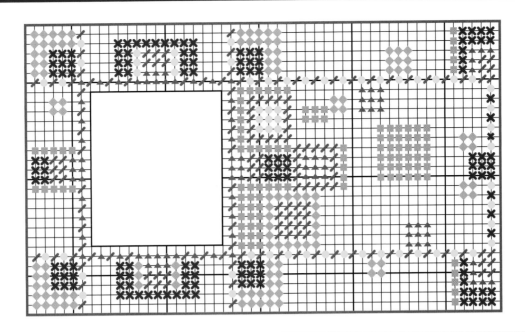

Colorway I
(black, pink, pearl)

Anchor 6-strand floss		Kreinik #16 med braid
#895 Rose	╱	
#1019 Deep Burgundy	✖	
#1020 Pink	◆	
#403 Black	☐	
	▲	#024 Fuchsia
	●	#042 Confetti Fuchsia (multi)
	■	#095 Starburst

Overcast outside edges of paperweight and inner frame edge
#095 Starburst Kreinik #16˝ ribbon

Colorway II
(blue, brown, rust)

Anchor 6-strand floss		Kreinik #16 med braid
#351 Dark Rust	╱	
#381 Dark Brown	✖	
#1048 Tan	◆	
#849 Blue	☐	
	▲	#021HL Copper
	●	#018HL Navy
	■	#032 Pearl

Overcast outside edges of paperweight and inner frame edge
#018 Navy Kreinik #16˝ ribbon

Colorway III
(red, yellow, blue)

Anchor 6-strand floss		Kreinik #16 med braid
#19 Red	╱	
#134 Blue	✖	
#298 Yellow	◆	
#158 Pale Blue	☐	
	▲	#091 Star Yellow (pale)
	●	#028 Citron (bright)
	■	#014 Sky Blue

Overcast outside edges of paperweight and inner frame edge
#003 Red Kreinik #16˝ ribbon

About The Author

Judi Kauffman is a versatile and prolific craft and needlework designer whose favorite techniques include needlepoint, quilting, bead embellishment, rubber stamping, crochet, and all kinds of embroidery. Born into a family of artists who made everything from scratch, she has been stitching, knitting, and sewing since she was small.

Judi has an undergraduate degree in printmaking from Cornell University and a master's degree in fibers from Antioch University. She has taught drawing, graphic design, illustration, and other studio courses at the college level for thirty years. She has taught needlepoint for the last eight years. Her background also includes graphic design, window displays, courtroom sketching, and teaching elementary and high school art.

Judi considers it her life's mission to convince people that they are creative, a goal that has led her to write and design for a wide variety of craft and needlework magazines, to write and produce videos, and develop kits for manufacturers. She wrote this book to encourage and nurture the packrat tendencies in others and to justify her own penchant for saving everything - from photographs, hankies, and old keys to the messages that come in fortune cookies and the canceled stamps on her mail.

Judi lives near Washington, D.C., with her minimalist husband (who is in charge of a very sparsely furnished living room) and an energetic poodle named Rudy (a patient companion in the studio, but a reincarnated aerobics teacher who keeps her moving the rest of the time).

Resources

Support your local craft and needlework retailer whenever possible. If you can't find the products and supplies you need, contact the manufacturers to locate a convenient store or mail order source.

API/Adhesive Products Inc.
Crafter's Pick Brush Strokes gloss finish
520 Cleveland Ave.
Albany, CA 94010
(510) 526-7616
http://www.crafterspick.com
www.crafterspick.com

Artemis Exquisite Embellishments
Hand-dyed bias cut silk ribbon
179 High St.
S. Portland, ME 04106
(207) 741-2509

Bagworks
Denim sling tote bag
3301-C So. Cravens Rd.
Fort Worth, TX 76119

Beacon Chemical Co.
Fabri-Tac, Gem-Tac, Kids Choice glues
Liquid Laminate available from Signature
PO Box 427
Wyckoff, NJ 07481
(800) 865-7238

Bucilla
Silk and organza ribbon, chenille needles, moiré fabric
One Oak Ridge Rd.
Hazleton, PA 18201
(800) 233-3239

Charles Craft
Cross-stitch fabrics
PO Box 1049
Laurenberg, NC 28353
(800) 277-1009

Clearsnap
Colorbox inks, Magic Stamp (PenScore) moldable foam blocks
PO Box 98
Anacortes, WA 98221
(800) 448-4862

Coats & Clark
Anchor 6-strand embroidery floss, crochet yarns
Consumer Service
PO Box 12229
Greenville, SC 26912
(800) 648-1479

Darice
Plastic canvas, alphabet beads
21160 Drake Rd.
Stronsville, OH 44136
(800) 321-1494

DMC
6-strand floss, Medicis, 3-ply Persian wool
South Hacksensack Ave.
Port Kearney Bldg 10A
S. Kearney, NJ 07032
(800) 275-4117

Dritz.
Fray Check, St. Jane Collection muslin sewing box
PO Box 5028
Spartanburg, SC 29304
(800) 845-4948

Duncan Enterprises
Aleene's Premium Coat Acrylic Paints, 3-D Accents design paste, create your own design template, trowels and design tool
5673 E. Shields Ave.
Fresno, CA 93727
(800) 237-2642

ETI/Environmental Technologies Inc.
Enviro-Tex Lite pour-on polymer coating
South Bay Depot Rd.
Fields Landing, CA 95537
(800) 368-9323

Fairfield Processing
Soft Touch pillow inserts
Box 1130
Danbury, CT 06813
(800) 980-8000

Fiskars
Paper crimper, 45mm rotary cutter with deckle blade, decorative paper edgers
PO Box 8027
Wausau, WI 54402
(800) 950-0203

HTC/Handler Textile Corp.
Fun-dation translucent quilt block piecing material, Quilt-Fuse, fleece and fusible fleece, Crafter's Choice iron-on stabilizer
60 Metro Way
Seacaucus, NJ 07094
Toll free (877) 448-2669

Hues, Inc.
Photo Effects fabric photo transfer papers for color copier and home computer
PO Box 190
Anderson, IN 46015
(800) 268-9841

Husqvarna Viking
Viking 1+ embroidery/sewing machine
11760 Berea Rd.
Cleveland, OH 44111
http://www.husqvarnaviking.com

Jesse James and Co.
Dress It Up assortments, buttons, charms, bows and dimensional embellishments
615 N. New St.
Allentown, PA 18102
(610) 435-7899

JHB International
Teddy bear, dove, acorns, trees, birds, teacups, and cardinal buttons; Angel Gabriel pins
1955 S. Quince St.
Denver, CO 80231
(303) 751-8100

Kreinik Mfg. Co., Inc.
Metallic braid and ribbon, torsade, Facets, silk
3106 Timanus La., Suite 101
Baltimore, MD 21244
(800) 624-1428

Krylon
Spray paint, Make It Suede
Available at your local paint and craft store

Mangelsen's
Velvet leaves and assorted embellishments
Available at your local craft and needlework retailer

McGill Creativity
1/16" hole punch, decorative paper punches and scissors
131 E. Prairie St.
Marengo, IL 60152
Customer service
(800) 654-6114

Microfleur
Microwave flower press
PO Box 280
Minden, NV 89423
(775) 265-2409

Mill Hill
*Crystal and Glass Treasures;
seed, bugle and pebble beads;
painted frames; gold pendant*
PO Box 1060
Janesville, WI 53547
(800) 356-9438

National ArtCraft Co.
Paintable watches
7996 Darrow Rd.
Twinsburg, OH 44087
Toll free (888) WE-R-
CRAFT

National Nonwovens
70% wool felt
PO Box 150
Easthampton, MA 01027
(800) 333-3469

Needle Necessities, Inc.
*Over-dyed 6-strand embroi-
dery floss, over-dyed French
wool*
72 11 Garden Grove Blvd.
#BC
Garden Grove, CA 92841
(714) 892-9211

Offray
Wire-edge ribbons
Available at your local craft
and needlework retailer

Personal Stamp Exchange
*Handmade paper cards,
blank cards and envelopes*
360 Sutton Pl.
Santa Rosa, CA 95407
(707) 588-8058

Plaid Enterprises, Inc.
Raffia Accents
PO Box 7600
Norcross, GA 30091
(770) 923-8200

Pleasant Recollections
*Vintage postcards, florals,
and graphics on synthetic
silk or canvas*
PO Box 1539
Wimberley, TX 78676
(800) 318-8391

Porcelain Rose
Rooster pin (recipe pocket)
PO Box 7545
Long Beach, CA 90807
(562) 427-2349

Ranger Industries
DecorIt inks
15 Park Rd.
Tinton Falls, NJ 07724
(732) 389-3535

Ribbon Connections
*Wide, sheer ribbons; ruffled
ribbon satin ribbon*
2971 Tea Garden St.
San Leandro, CA 94577

Ruban et Fleur
*Vintage velvet leaves, buds,
foliage, ribbons, trims*
8655 S. Sepulveda Blvd.
Los Angeles, CA 90045
(310) 641-3466

Sakura of America
*Micron Pigma, Brush and
Callipen for paper and fabric*
30780 San Clemente St.
Hayward, CA 94544
(800) 776-6257

Savage Universal
Pre-cut mats
550 East Elliott Rd.
Chandler, AZ 85225
(602) 632-1320

Scratch Art
*3D-O's dimensional 2-side
adhesive dots*
PO Box 303
Avon, MA 02322
(800) 377-9003

Sticker Planet
*Stickers, pre-cut corrugated
cardboard frames*
10736 Jefferson Blvd.
Culver City, CA 90230
(800) 557-8678

Sudberry House
*Collector's cabinet, memory
trays, ring boxes, music
jewelry box, oval moiré box,
square black wood box*
PO Box 895
Old Lyme, CT 06371
(800) 243-2607

Sulyn Industries
Pearls and pastel pearls
11927 W. Sample Rd.
Coral Springs, FL 33065

Sweet Child of Mine
*Hand-dyed silk ribbon (ring
box project)*
139 E. Fremont Ave.
Sunnyvale, CA 94087
(408) 720-8426

The Shell Factory
Shells, shells, shells
2787 N. Tamiami Trail
N. Ft. Meyers, FL 33903
Toll free (888) 4SHELLS.

ThermOWeb
*Peel'n Stick double sided
adhesive sheet*
770 Glenn Ave.
Wheeling, IL 60090
(847) 520-5200

Tsukineko
*Dauber Duos, Encore
Ultimate Metallic rubber
stamp inks*
15411 NE 95th St.
Redmond, WA 98052
(800) 769-6633

Uchida of America
Marvy fabric markers
36 Steeplechase Rd.
Millstone Twp.
Robbinsville, NJ 08691
(609) 443-4712

Voice Express
*Voice recordable greeting
cards, recordable modules for
frames and stuffed toys*
42 Oak Ave.
Tuckahoe, NY 10707
Toll free (888) 293-5855

The Warm Co.
Pre-quilted muslin
954 East Union St.
Seattle, WA 98122
(800) 234-9276

Wimpole Street Creations
*Dish towel, fabric yo yos,
crochet flowers*
Available from Barrett
House
PO Box 540585
North Salt Lake, UT 84054
(801) 299-0700

Wrights
*Pre-made ribbon rosettes and
buds*
Available at your local craft
and needlework retailer

Xyron
*Models #850 and #1250 (for
place mats) laminating and
adhesive application
machines*
14698 North 78th Way
Scottsdale, AZ 85260

Yarn Tree
*Snow globes, glass paper-
weights*
PO Box 724
Ames, IA 50010
(800) 247-3952

Preserve Your Memories

MORE THAN MEMORIES

The Complete Guide For Preserving Your Family History

Edited by Julie Stephani

Leading scrapbook experts share hundreds of their favorite tips and techniques to instruct and inspire you to create beautiful family albums that will be cherished for generations to come! Clear step-by-step instructions show you how to organize, protect, and display your treasured photos. Improve your journaling skills and choose from many different styles of lettering to match any theme.

Softcover • 8½ x 11 • 128 pages
225 color photos
MTM • $14.95

Editor Julie Stephani

MORE THAN MEMORIES II

Beyond the Basics

Edited by Julie Stephani

Scrapbook experts share new and creative techniques for preserving your family memories. The second book in the series goes beyond the basics to include step-by-step instructions on photo tinting, paper embossing, and photo transferring, as well as ideas on making greeting cards, puzzles, and time capsules. There are still plenty of great page layout ideas on thirteen favorite themes, including Heritage, Home and Family, Babies, Vacations, Weddings, and much more.

Softcover • 8½ x 11 • 128 pages
200 color photos
MTMB • $16.95

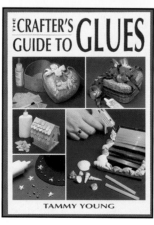